BARBWIRE NOOSE®

FEAR IS THE ROOT OF ALL WEAKNESS®

MAKE WORLDS

Fear Is The Root of All Weakness®

Marcia Anita Hobbs

MARCIA BNOOSE

ANYTHING BUT ORDINARY

Judgement and Perception have NO value here. ©

AUTOBIOGRAPHICAL SERIES

ABOUT THE AUTHOR

Human Rights Activist Marcia BNoose.

Author, born as Marcia Anita Hobbs in Rose Park, Adelaide, South Australia, 25th April 1984.

In 2015, Le Droit Humain Co-Freemasonry, Lodge 406.

When the most Honest thing you can ever say is the Oddest thing you will ever say… "I wouldn't change a day or have it any other way." – Marcia Anita Hobbs, aka Marcia B. Noose, "Anything But Ordinary." – Judgment and Perception Have No Value Here; Autobiographical Series.

The content of this is Real. Candid, clumsy, courageous, and curious. Enjoy x

DEDICATION

To everyone I love and to Justice for All.

For everyone who believes in the Universal Declaration of Human Rights, shall Good always prevail over evil.

A Better World. To Justice for All. Truth Matters.

This Series of Books.

Autobiographies, A Brand Dedicated To 'A Better World' – Human Rights. The Autobiographical Series 'Anything But Ordinary – Judgement And Perception Have No Value Here' is a collection of books full of candid facts, Experiences, Quotes, and open to Interpretation, depending on where the Reader's head is at – Judgment, Education, My Life, And Thoughts. Stories Of The Heart, Mind, and Soul, Consisting Of Personal Views, knowledge, and life experiences, as well as light-hearted, Comedic References, Poetry, World facts, and More.

Quoting A Letter To Professor Fatima Meer From The Book 'Conversations With Myself' By Nelson Mandela: "The Trouble, Of Course, Is That Most Successful Men Are Prone To Some Form Of Vanity. There Comes A Stage In Their Lives When They Consider It Permissible To Be Egotistic And To Brag To The Public At Large About Their Unique Achievements. What a Sweet Euphemism for Self-Praise the English Language Has Evolved! Autobiography, They Choose To Call It, Where The Shortcomings Of Others Are Frequently Exploited To Highlight The Praiseworthy Accomplishments Of The Author."

As a true crime writer and author of biographical literature, I Could Relate To Nelson Mandela's View of Autobiography. Although I

Have Ensured That My Life's Evolution, in Its Imperfections and Perfections, has been Equally Shared, I cannot help but feel at Times That the Personal Nature of my autobiographies has truthfully. Graphically Shared the Shortcomings Of Others, Not Just My Own. Being Mindful Not To Brag Yet Proud Of My Achievements, This Euphemism Interpretation Is Bang On The Realities Of A Biographical Record. The Highs And The Lows Of Life, Often Shared Moments. When The Hunter Talks Of Killing The Lion, It Is The Hunter's Life That Is Glorified, Though The Lion Has Great Achievements Of Its Own Unshared, As A Hunter Only KnowS His Own Life And The Lion's Role In It.

Human Rights Matter

ANYTHING BUT ORDINARY –
JUDGMENT AND PERCEPTION HAVE NO VALUE HERE.

BOOK NO. 2

(of however many books in the series I would like)

CHAPTERS

THE REBELLION

"Here's to the crazy ones. The misfits. The rebels. The troublemakers. The round pegs in the square holes. The ones who see things differently. They're not fond of rules. And they have no respect for the status quo. You can quote them, disagree with them, glorify, or vilify them. About the only thing you can't do is ignore them. Because they change things. They push the human race forward. And while some may see them as the crazy ones, we see genius. Because the people who are crazy enough to think they can change the world, are the ones who do."- Rob Siltanen

FUN SHIT

Live - Laugh - Love.

PIECES OF AUSTRALIA (THROUGH MY EYES)

The list is at times long; all I can say is he was "A few stubbies short of a six-pack."

PIECES OF ME

Things you may know or may not know about me.

HISTORY

"Those who cannot remember the past are condemned to repeat it."
– George Santayana, The Life of Reason, 1905, from the series Great Ideas of Western Man.

Which is EXACTLY what some historical accounts want.

MAKING MUSIC

Hell and Sunshine, that's how you taste - Tantalising.

POETRY

Poems by yours truly.

PROTEST

A statement or action expressing disapproval of or objection to something. "The team lodged an official protest".

TRUTH VS LIES

Be careful what lies you tell about me; some dick heads may be corrected in these books. Defamation is costly. Perjury is a crime in Australia, carrying a penalty of up to four years' incarceration.

REAL TALK - AUSTRALIA'S MOST INFAMOUS WHISTLEBLOWER

Half of a paedophile protection racket consisting of police, sub-standard bikers, and overall shit humans refuted my whistleblowing with perjury. Everyone else loved me or didn't care. Personally, I've never really cared too much about other people's opinions to bother me. Defamation should be compensated; bullshit can be ignored.

FREEMASONRY

"That a man be willing, when others are so too, as far forth as for peace and defence of himself he shall think it necessary, to lay down this right to all things; and be contented with so much liberty against other men, as he would allow other men against himself." - Thomas Hobbes

OPINIONS AND RANDOM SH*T

Opinions are like assholes: everyone has one—these are mine. Plus, Anything but Ordinary random shit.

Contents

Introduction

When the most Honest thing you can ever say is the oddest thing you will ever say… "I wouldn't change a day or have it any other way." – Marcia BNoose (Hobbs)

The Anything but Ordinary Autobiographical Series is a collective of extracts from the Heart, Time, and Mind.

Enjoy x

Chapter One
'The Rebellion'

I hope this series of books and its autobiographical content are a little light-hearted, like me, happy-go-lucky. And above all, an honest account of my simple yet extraordinary life thus far. Although some chapters outline the profound impact that whistleblowing has had on my life and survival, this ongoing series of books is more focused on the beauty and absurdity of life.

"Here's to the crazy ones. The misfits. The rebels. The troublemakers. The round pegs in the square holes. The ones who see things differently. They're not fond of rules. And they have no respect for the status quo. You can quote them, disagree with them, glorify, or vilify them. About the only thing you can't do is ignore them. Because they change things, they push the human race forward. And while some may see them as the crazy ones, we see genius. Because the people who are crazy enough to think they can change the world are the ones who do."- Rob Siltanen

To me, this statement is rebel. It's a plot twist —the overthrow: We the People, You and Me.

I've been a rebel against authority since I was a teenager. Standing up against false narratives, bullies, and in defence of individuals or causes, as well as for people's rights, is my norm.

In this book, I have dedicated a chapter to active protest, whether it is through a petition or by standing on the steps of parliament. These are civil ways of generating accountability and change. In this chapter, I briefly touch on what I call the rebellion— civil disobedience in response to oppression, harassment, and torture inflicted by the government to cover up its actions.

For centuries, civil disobedience has been the foundation of change in the face of tyrannical government litigation and has enhanced communities for The People. It is usually enacted by one person, followed by others. A single person's choice to stand up against bias, yet accepted narratives, racism, dictatorships, etc. This chapter is not overly light-hearted. Nor is the chapter' Truth vs. Lies.' Full of facts and extracts, if you have read UGLY HEROS Autobiography, you will know some of these things. If you had read book one of this Anything But Ordinary (ABO) series, you would have a broad understanding of some of this book series' contents.

"Views change, we grow, we learn, we improve, but one thing is constant, and that is the truth. Never stop evolving just because others want to hold you back to the old, the expired, their bullshit." Marcia BNoose (Marcia Anita Hobbs)

Anything But Ordinary

I was unstoppable in 2022, really. The Truth was irrefutable, and the lies literally showed themselves to anyone who cared about the truth. More so with the truth in black and white by the beginning of 2023, though you only knew this if you were close to me or bothered reading, which most didn't do. Surprised by this, I pursued justice and the truth to no end. The defamatory game the government had run against me was not over, but it was won in the courts. Police had been unable to legally take me to court for anything related to my role as a good Samaritan and upstanding member of the public for years. A reputation I was able to maintain, just. It was shocking how very few people are really interested in the truth if they can benefit from the lies. In 2025, I put in serious effort to refute the perceptive narrative, especially after my living situation revealed a history of rape and domestic violence tendencies. Conspire against me for paedophiles at your own peril – Judgement and Perception have NO Value Here.

The plot of police efforts to cover up sex offending, including paedophilia, thickened with every intentional, malicious accusation made against my character. The efforts by police forces and government to distort the truth and disrupt my safety were as endless as the decades of abuses of power and process that they so desperately wanted to hide—a totalitarian regime. Police officers encouraged and committed blatant perjury in a cover-up operation to pervert the course of justice and bring the administration of justice into disrepute.

Totalitarian / ˌtəʊtalɪˈtɛːrɪən,tə(ʊ)ˌtalɪˈtɛːrɪən/adjective

relating to a system of government that is centralised and dictatorial and requires complete subservience to the state. "a totalitarian regime"

Subservience; noun: subserviency - willingness to obey others unquestioningly.

Damages by 2022 were astronomical, let alone those that would follow. To my surprise, the police forces of Australia played the illegal card and acted on the malpractice and maladministration of a known criminal employed by VICPOL. Actions that continued beyond 2024 under an irrefutably venal federal Labor government, led by Anthony Albanese. The Labor government was responsible for criminal negligence regarding disabled persons and police operations surrounding me. Many police forces, knowing what I know, I think must have quietly rejoiced in the newly elected national government, which led the way for paedophilia cover-ups with the unconstitutional association laws introduced in 2008 under the Labor Mike Rann government. Mike Rann is known publicly for his association with paedophilia and his part in grooming young men for notorious sex offender Bevan Spencer von Einem. However, SAPOL has never charged the ex-state parliament leader for grooming at least. Recorded offences, even discussed with a Flinders University researcher, claim brave and honest victims of Bevan Spencer von Einem—sad truths. Reality is, how could SAPOL charge government officials – especially officials with power over them, when the police had been engaging in the same level of sexual crimes.

All this public online — The Story Behind the Brand BARBWIRE NOOSE® global by 2023 — it seemed that nothing but the media's involvement would stop the abomination of a cover-up. Meanwhile, the press was like crickets on all this government departmental criminal negligence and the cover-up. Media always floated around in the background, surrounding me, getting lost in the most damaging cover-up in Australian history—at least the most widely documented and publicly disclosed. Australia's national security was compromised entirely by paedophile offences and sex crimes, which flooded law enforcement, the defence force, and leading ministerial roles.

The police were desperate, the government was desperate, and the petty criminals and gossips were desperate too – all needed the defamation, their perjury to permeate to benefit.

Personally, as a developing whistle-blower (if that's something!) since the age of nineteen, I foresaw that police forces would do the wrong thing and compromise my life, thinking they were running a successful cover-up before settling torts. And I was right. Inductive reasoning – using past experiences to make future predictions is natural, logical, and inductive philosophy.

I had a lawyer. I always had a lawyer. Usually, communicating with numerous lawyers at once. Nearly always, my legal representation failed to act in my best interests. Cooperated with malicious accusations; in this torts case beginning in 2022, my legal representation allowed the unreasonable administrative delays by the government agency VICPOL and the Freedom of Information (FOI) office, resulting in their failure to complete my torts claim. Torts are pursued through court proceedings, and tort actions are acknowledged by the judge, resulting in a winning tort claim that is undisputable.

The fact that VICPOL delayed and refused to release the perjury information in my FOI, and failed to release the FOI within a specified time frame, over three years of non-disclosure of my FOI and court audio, I am entitled to. An abuse of process. The fact that my legal representation (Aussie Lawyers) failed to settle these torts and seemingly abandoned representation altogether is a violation of their legal responsibilities and of my rights to a fair trial in these matters. The withholding of FOI and court records – intentional justice delayed; unduly delayed can be rightly labelled a deliberate act of perjury. Due process violations, among other delay tactics used by law enforcement, including lying under oath, perversion of justice, and malfeasance, are at the top of the cover-up checklist.

After I obtained a lawyer, before they abandoned the case, police torts escalated to the point where I was falsely incarcerated.

Falsely incarcerated, the time allowed me to build a stronger case against VICPOL. Over twenty days felt like a month. Falsely imprisoned for twenty-three days, I documented all the illegal activities, including property theft, inadequate time out of my cell, and withholding of medication, and reported them through the appropriate channels before blowing the whistle on the Victorian government-run jail.

Dame Phyllis Frost Centre (DPFC) employed many ex-VICPOL members; some staff were genuinely concerned for my welfare, but most were trying their best to make this false incarceration period hard-time for me, even though I was placed in media protection, the protection unit of DPFC. Police directly threatened my safety inside DPFC as I pursued a central tort claim and criminal charges against police – not a coincidence—the courts of Victoria's actions aiding and abetting a plot by VICPOL to endanger my life detrimentally. The decision of remand instead of bail by the male judge on the nineteenth of August 2023 was complicit in an effort to push the refuge of suicide or worse, an assassination plot, with death in jail being a possible result.

VICPOL, irrefutably, with the intention to spread malicious defamation and perjury, intended to cause me harm while incarcerated. I repeat that I spoke out in court, stating the punishment of remand was excessive, which the judge acknowledged on the fifth of September 2022 upon my release—a decade of police recklessly endangering my life by circulating malicious accusations with no basis or facts of sex industry work, escalating to claims that I 'dated' cops, and damaging claims of an informant status while I was arbitrarily detained—damages amounting to an uncompensable level of damage. My time, a month, and the Barbwire Noose® New York Fashion Week (NYFW) 2022 opportunity are unredeemable. Uncompensable costs to my reputation, business, and safety that I somehow needed to sum up a settlement price for. Not naive to the fact that Aussie Lawyers were not a household Australian firm name for a reason. Governance is willing to cost the taxpayers millions and waste millions of taxpayers' dollars on a cover-up. Yet my suffering at the hands of a police sex offender and government corruption would be reinvested into the economy viably. Thinking resolution, the process would be less costly overall if settled outside of court. Although I wanted it all documented on court records, I was happy to go to court, just not excited about making a big deal out of it. Especially when the damages amount to losing numerous opportunities to attend NYFW and to the intentional commission of further malicious torts. The settlement of these torts and the cover-up were delayed, resulting in the loss of three NYFW opportunities as NYFW 2023 passed, and perjury continued to circulate in Australia and abroad. I had thought about resolution a lot over the years that I witnessed the police cover-up of sex crimes. The total overall, including charges and all facets, with government departments held accountable through the courts, is in the billions. The multi-millions spent on the cover-up set the bar for the enormity of my suffering.

Upon my release from DPFC, I was ready to update my autobiographies and follow up on the reports to governing bodies, which I did. The truth circulated the globe, free to download from the National Library of Australia, and was available to borrow at The British Library, before VICPOL settled on irrefutable torts – before compensation for torts engaged for a paedophile cover-up hit my bank. The shamelessness of both men and women employed in law enforcement and government who were failing to act on sexual misconduct and institutional abuse is a display of contemptible cowardice and a despicable lack of morality.

I knew this was going to be a me versus DPFC and VICPOL regarding their alleged illegality. When the date passed, September 5, 2023, without a torts settlement – a year after the judge stated I should not have been incarcerated - it was irrefutable that the Australian Federal Police (AFP) had been complicit and directly involved in the torts. Both Reece Kershaw, the AFP Commissioner, and Commissioner Shane Patton of VICPOL, amongst the numerous police commissioners, were seemingly happy to conspire on some level and drown in the venal state of the governmental and law enforcement cover-up of paedophilia and its endless malfeasance. Stealing justice from vulnerable Australians (disabled persons) as police officers for paedophilia, I am not sure that police forces can go much lower than this. And if they were willing to stoop lower, public disclosure ensured history was not covered up, at least as I continued to write and fight the good fight.

The Melbourne detention centre (DPFC) was as dehumanising as the experiences I had with police covering up paedophilia, a cesspool of human rights violations, sexual indiscretions – numerous general crimes act violations like drug dealing, as well as negligence of the duty e.g. deprivations of medication, which both SAPOL and NSWPOL were already guilty of, plus theft, reckless endangerment, criminal negligence, perjury, and sexual misconduct (not limited to).

I went through the motions of reporting to managers and the ombudsman while falsely incarcerated; I might as well report. If need be, publicly disclose and whistle-blow to all related government departments and sectors involved in the torts, I thought. Not surprisingly, little changed over nearly two years. VICPOL and DPFC employees stole my property and damaged my property in an intentional and malicious attempt to cause further emotional harm, financial suffering, and damages, as well as conspired to endanger my life recklessly. Blatant perjury and criminal conduct by VICPOL in hopes I would lose my life due to their malicious, illegal operations, and /or seek the refuge of suicide. Actions clearly supported by the AFP led by Reece Kershaw – irrefutable after nearly two years of unsettled torts, and the AFP Commissioner was more than aware of my name and surrounding circumstances. I was deprived of liberties, deprived of a safe place, deprived of my property, etc. Enduring endless criminal act violations and Human Rights violations, arbitrarily arrested, and detained, as with my property. Actions which were then repeated by criminal members of the public who proclaimed alliances with police, business people, freemasons, felons, and accused sex offenders, all engaged in acts of deprivation in hopes of benefiting from the government covering up sex crimes. The choice to incarcerate myself was based on random choice or personal whim, rather than any reason or system, "an arbitrary decision". An arbitrary decision made by police to abuse power and process (malpractice and maladministration), the judge complied, as I clearly stated in court before I was falsely incarcerated, that this punishment would exceed any just consequence that could stem from the illegal charges. On August 19, 2022, in the Melbourne Magistrates' Court, the judge denied bail based on historical false charges for which I was never convicted. NSW Courts had engaged in the same behaviour. The Victoria court judge stated that the court did not have time to hear the case after numerous persons who had been in custody for less time than I were passed through the court ahead of me. Further evidence that the justice system is already in disrepute due to constitutional law violations, as well as a failure of separation of powers, allowing this injustice to occur initially, can be seen in this attitude to judgment, an attitude shared in all courts I faced during torts in South Australia, New South Wales, and Victoria.

VICPOL took 35 weeks to release Freedom of Information (FOI) documents in response to my request. A process breaching constitutional rights to a fair trial. The legal maxim 'justice delayed is justice denied' is an essential element of a cover-up. The AFP has failed to charge police officers with their involvement in Organised crime since 2014, and continues to do so, adding a further tort claim that I would need to litigate against the venal AFP. The AFP witness too and part of the process that arbitrarily deprived me of my freedom, officers wilfully contributing to the abuse of power and process. This was evident after nearly a year had passed from the false incarceration. After almost two years had passed, the acknowledged court tort settlement had not been settled. It was abandoned by my legal representation—a clear win that was abandoned, definitely something to see here. The CIA in the background pretending they were judge and jury – freemason and nazi, which saw me lose respect for a fickle bunch of power-tripping men that needed to be investigated and charged by the FBI. Perjury out of control, analytics technology abuses engaged in espionage, and a decade of sex driven and deprived men surrounding me was fucking ridiculous and fucking up civil society as we know it. Just look at the Epstein and Maxwell saga, Guilty as charged, yet apparently no one is a victim, what's that if not a cover-up of elite sexual screw ups.

The unjust perversion of justice regarding an acknowledged court tort occurred when the FOI unit withheld my FOI request for 35 weeks, allowing VICPOL, with the assistance of the AFP and fellow corrupt individuals with vested interests, time to disrupt my life further while police forces worked to prevent my attendance at NYFW2023. I was seeking over five million dollars in settlement for reward money, plus compensation for the assistance and reckless use of my life. Regarding the most severe emotional distress, including torts, personal injuries/redress claims, compensation for intentional and malicious efforts, including perjury, and damages since 2012, with the immeasurable loss of NYFW opportunities. This sum, calculated based on damages, potential earnings, taxpayers' money invested in the cover-up, and the extraordinary emergency circumstances and suffering I endured, is priceless. VICPOL and SAPOL to pay the exact total of five million dollars each for intel is cheap labour. The federal compensation sum should exceed both states' investments in the cover-up and must include the perjury committed by political parties. Willing to go to court for resolution, I acknowledge that this process will likely carry further emotional distress, which should be compensated. 'Happy' is probably an inappropriate description of my overall attitude towards resolving an irrefutable and court-acknowledged tort.

My emotional distress was overwhelming, and life-threatening circumstances reached a level at which I should have died. I spent a lot of money on medicinal marijuana (cannabis) in 2023 and thereafter. The government prescribed it, and I knew exactly what I was getting. The process is an absolute bullshit head fuck, I strongly feel the government should not be the regulator of a natural seed that has suffered decades of oppressive legislation, though broadly known for its medical treatment. The only good thing about medical weed is that you know exactly what you are getting. I based my therapy on comparing strains to those that I had commonly smoked for years. Cannabis is my long-term 101 for dealing with life's stresses. I took the medicinal use thing seriously until the end of 2023, when I was over this medicinal treatment being used as a mental health excuse for lying under oath by police. Personally, I knew how to deal with my CPTSD. I had been in this state of complex trauma recovery since I was sixteen years old. I wanted the antidepressant to calm my emotions and avoid collapsing from stress for the third time in as many years. Fainting in 2021 and 2022 from stress, the 2022 collapse was in public and in front of two children, to whom I felt sorry, who had to witness the state to which my health had been reduced. Most strains prescribed were over twenty per cent THC. They did enough to help me deal with the stress without smoking every day or excessively, like I did in 2019/2020 with court proceedings surrounding my statement against police paedophile Kurt Slaven. Still smoking heavily, yet just a gram of medical marijuana per day, which was bittersweet.

The best way I could refute false narratives and perceptions was to write. Great therapy too. The counsellor's agreement with my writing was excellent. Lawyers acknowledged my legal research and case references, which demonstrated that my book was well-written. Judges encouraged my pursuit of my talents, and publishers praised and published my books. Writing became my Rebellion. I still had to fight to see justice for the sex crimes committed against me as a minor and for the cover-up of crimes against persons with the self-defence capacity of an infant, but it could no longer be covered up, not with the truth written and me still writing.

My family would be partly responsible for the loss of my life in criminal negligence (if I died). SAPOL, perjury, and my parents' contribution to my house being illegally acquired are the leading causes of the most damage and assaults to occur during severe reckless endangerment. Reckless endangerment in an extraordinary emergency, which had mounted for over ten years, by police forces. There has been no real safe place for me to live since 2016. I do not doubt the level of responsibility police forces are accountable for regarding how much the public knows about their perjury; the anomalies are irrefutable. My parents had been inconsistent in their support of my pursuit of justice since the beginning. Time does not heal all wounds. Subject to endless investigations into nothing, so that police could pervert the course of justice for sex offenders. I found very little relief from malicious intentions and perjury for over half a decade, being forced to seek new residences because everyone joined the small-minded gossip. The bigotry of the human race is the reason for every war ever started and fought. And it was everywhere, government haters were bigots (which was weird), hippies were bigots, the LGBTQ community were bigots, even those in the disabilities sector work held beliefs and arrogant opinions which diminished justice for all, diminished Human rights. The lows of man will never surprise me. I never regretted the fight, but I did regret giving respect to many people who ultimately deserved a smack in the head. Some are so hopeless in life that they could not afford the defamation and perjury they spread, and cared not for the disabled persons to whom they were depriving justice altogether. Such ignorance only learns from violence, sadly, dominated by the primal mentality of dog-eat-dog. The lack of a logical rationale is often frustrating, which is why the endless memes about idiots remind us of our like-mindedness on social media.

I had spent years counteracting numerous disruptions to Barbwire Noose®, which had cost the brand excessively in damages and ensured profits remained low due to a constant need to invest in reputational Public Relations. Brand Barbwire Noose on a limited budget against the government and law enforcement budgets – the government's investment in a cover-up via the misappropriation of taxpayers' funds seems to be a multimillion-dollar venture. Despite my personal efforts to get on with life, perjury fell on feeble ears more often than not, and devastated justice for both disabled people and myself, as explained in the legal maxim that justice delayed is justice denied. Julian Assange, knowing the lack of boundaries regarding injustices allowed towards whistle-blowers, well. The incarceration, all the institutional ongoings felt next-level – Assange-level oppression.

I had been cast as an extra in a series starring icon actress Sigourney Weaver, an SBS and Netflix aired four-episode Australian series 'True Colours', as well as cast as lead actor for a state-wide television advertisement in the Northern Territory in 2022 (before false incarceration). Featuring in three of the four episodes of 'True Colours' aired on Netflix, and made the most-watched across Australia in 2023. These acting roles filmed before VICPOL, NSWPOL, and the AFP, plus other police forces, maliciously engaged in incarceration torts in a cover-up of sex offending, including paedophilia. If I were being investigated at this time for any accusations – malicious or pending, the police would have on record my acting roles. They would be aware of the damages they were intentionally causing by acting on perjury and false statements to cover up sex crimes. Irrefutably, I was deliberately and maliciously incarcerated, causing further tort litigation action from me against VICPOL. My lawyer, Aussie Lawyers, at this time was aiding and abetting torts of emotional distress, allowing my life to be obstructed by delays and by not taking legal action in my best interests, like an application of mandamus writ against SAPOL and further litigation actions against VICPOL, which were my instructions. Especially considering the courts had acknowledged that I should not have been incarcerated solely based on text messages – a conclusion that settles the tort claim without the need for court proceedings or a determination by the Integrity Commission (IBAC Victoria/ICAC South Australia). Pro-bono is rarely a dedicated legal action for the average income earner (aka whistle-blower) against the government. Lawyers become afraid, at the least regarding losing legal aid favours. After years of being dicked around by lawyers as police tried to justify sex crimes with claims of prostitution and mental instability, I had had enough of the attitudes of litigation and the severe compromise to the justice system of Australia due to departmental lack of separation of powers – institutional abuse. Luckily, as a legal student myself, I was able to utilise statutory declarations and legal documents to mount a legal defence against defamation, provide evidence to integrity bodies, and arrange litigation. This did not stop police perjury, though.

The advert filmed was a mental health campaign for recovery, the EASA counselling service TVC filmed before my being falsely incarcerated and aired upon my release. I seriously could have benefited from a meditation session or two with these guys after such a vile, violating, and humiliating experience of false incarceration. The TVC, scheduled to air for much of 2023, was rumoured to be filmed on both television and internet-based platforms. The Lost Flowers of Alice Hart, starring well-known actresses Sigourney Weaver and Asher Keddie, an Australian actress, is a global television series based on a famous book, aired on Prime TV in August 2023. My barista colleague and I were blurred in the background in Episode 6 during the cafe scene.

It seemed evident that no matter how hard I worked, the damage caused by malicious accusations with no basis or facts was detrimental wherever I travelled in Australia. Beyond my ability to repair, I stayed above water, just. Still, I did not prosper in Australia without police forces torts addressed under the Torture Act, Privacy and Security Act, Crimes Act, police disciplinary act, and substantial tort settlements. Without Kurt Slaven being charged, I repeatedly applied for a green card to move to New York, ensuring that if approved, my brand's attendance at New York Fashion Week

(NYFW) would only be disrupted until beyond NYFW 2025 – justice prevailing.

I was better off away from my venal and deceptive family, too, who benefited much at my expense when I was present in Australia. Everyone around me showed to be opportunistic at the expense of my welfare, with no concerns regarding the disabled persons' justice, the police, and the government were side-stepping with severe defamation, character assassination attempts to bury the truth. As 2023 passed, so did the immediate and easiest opportunity to obtain justice for those subject to criminal negligence in the disability sector under Jay Weatherill and Premier Mike Rann, with the Disability Royal Commission concluding on 15 September 2023.

The callousness of man gives life to the death of my soul. Feeling dead after false incarceration, losing my dignity to a sex offender's cover-up was unexplainable and soul-shaking, but gave way to the ultimate Rebellion. Liberation from social definition by the completely contrasting life I lived compared to the one that the police led people to believe. I let people think whatever for a while in mid-2023. Leaving the fools to be foolish, I corrected only a few lost souls and lived more so than usual by my own quote, "Judgement and perception have NO value here." Very liberating after years of counteractive measures aimed at subduing the narrative. Also short-lived, as SAPOL did not let up with sex worker allegations via retired and serving police personnel, which was irrefutable in August 2023, while I, for a short period, resided in Adelaide, South Australia, again by choice.

People will believe what suits them most of the time. After a decade of defamation from revenge porn, perjury, and police criminal negligence, I knew this was fact all too well – people will believe what they want to believe. When you realise the truth matters to a person, and that is obvious, then your interactions with the ignorant become less painful - I think anyway.

My OnlyFans account was revealed to be the subject of many Mount Gambier residents (not isolated to SA); malicious remarks implying sex work, pornography, etc. Some people tried to solicit me as a sex worker, which is actually illegal to offer someone money or a reward for sexual favours randomly. The implications of sex work prove the damages caused by SAPOL police and my family's perjury in a cover-up of sex offending. It was in writing that my occupation was not a prostitute on OnlyFans, as well as me putting a copyright litigation notice on my profile. People had no reason to engage with me on a promiscuous or sex worker level – no reason to believe that was what my OnlyFans account was about. This was irrefutably due to perjury. The fact that persons violated copyright law screenshotting and circulating pictures across my hometown, which felon and paedophile Luke Ryan of Mt Gambier, South Australia, forwarded to me in 2023, shows the level that persons were willing to go due to law enforcement allowing felons to circulate private material (revenge porn) for over a decade globally. A cover-up that I witnessed and can legally testify to under oath has been ongoing since at least 2016 and continues into 2024. A cover-up that commenced well before 2016. To be free from institutional governance abuse, the last course of resolution was the high courts; if public accountability was not enough, pursuing relevant criminal charges and civil litigation for compensation were my only options. I had been avoiding a High Court application, knowing the Australian High Court's function was led by the government. A fact irrefutable after the release of George Pell (Catholic Cardinal) under the liberal government of Scott Morrison. I also knew the High Court's resolution resulted in the harshest consequences for all involved in the cover-up, especially entrapment. Law enforcement has no defence regarding their engagement in entrapment. The facts surrounding me show irrefutable entrapment by law enforcement, which extends to international evidence of this crime.

For me, the damages were literally proven within the evident decline of my life, lifestyle, and personal status in the community since assisting the police force with the deliberately botched Gordon Tearonui Hamm homicide. A homicide investigation that proved Australian police forces were involved in dealing with ICE, organised crime, and murder.

When I opened an OnlyFans account, it was after I was repeatedly and excessively illegally strip-searched (mainly just stripped repeatedly) across two countries and a total of three states (international and Australian National). NSWPOL illegally strip-searched me on camera for both male and female guards to witness. This action caused me so much emotional distress that I struggled to eat even though I was starving, having survived nearly a week of false incarceration. I threw my pants at one of the female guards complaisant in this torture's harassment. The large female guard, enjoying the strip show, was threatening me for my rebellious behaviour. Once stripped, I stood there with my hands placed behind my head as the lesbian or lesbian wannabe gawked at me naked. This is all on camera. Incarcerated, I suffered from a severe lack of hygiene needs, personal care standards I was used to and deprived of, as well as a very questionable level of liberties supplied to a person not convicted of any crimes – myself, a humble Human Rights Activist. The OnlyFans account further solidified within many direct messages, that police covering up sex crimes with malicious accusations with no basis or facts, perjury regarding sex work, and myself were insurmountable without legal ramifications to all involved in an affray of defamation to benefit sex offenders. Knowing the damage from perjury was astronomical in my hometown of Mount Gambier, due to SAPOL's institutional harassment, which was acknowledged by Magistrate Teresa

Anderson in 2018 in a Mount Gambier Magistrates Court hearing, witnessed by lawyer John Kyrimis, and not amounting to a Royal Commission into SAPOL at this time?

OnlyFans revealed a lot within the seedy and unsavoury requests coming in from people I knew and others, evidence of the damage caused by police forces' shameful agenda. OnlyFans also further solidified police forces' entrapment pursuit. Directly correlated with SAPOL's institutional harassment, torts, countless false statements, and perjury.

Two of my Autobiographies were subjects of Royal Commissions (Disability and Domestic, Family and Sexual Violence), by 2025, I was broadly known and the public interest publications I had written when the seedy and unsavoury requests were made, was also broadly known. The solicitation and porn request came in on OnlyFans from people I knew, went to school with, locals where I grew up, Australians who had been party to the circulation of revenge porn (sprint cars associated personalities, etc), and military personnel, I had evidence of the police forces' perjury and shameful agenda of entrapment on an international platform.

Police forces maliciously collecting explicit and personal content from boyfriends and relations over the years and intentionally spreading much R-rated content, amongst many circles of society, proved out of control regarding both me and Barbwire

Noose, suffering reputational and across-the-board potential earnings damages.

In general, soliciting is banned in Australia under section 25 of the Summary Offences Act, punishable by a maximum penalty of a $750 fine. It is an offence to assist in, keep, or manage a brothel, as well as receive money paid in a brothel in respect of sex work, pursuant to section 28 (2022).

By definition, *Solicitation* is a noun.

1.   The act of asking for or trying to obtain something from someone.

"he was a regular target for solicitation of funds."

2.   The act of accosting someone and offering one's or someone else's services as a prostitute.

The police forces maliciously accused me of sex work, spread false rumours about sex work, and engaged in an act of solicitation (and entrapment), considering I was pursued in this manner directly from their perjury. Perjury carries a four-year incarceration term as a criminal offence—a direct result of law enforcement lying under oath, which by 2022 had undeniably spread damagingly across the globe.

One could argue the malicious accusations with no basis or facts recorded with the police, circulated to the point where they had engaged solicitation – offering myself in defamation as a prostitute to fellow police engaging with prostitutes, bikers, freemasons, and other persons, as I was pursued for sexual service and by sex work employment with bikers (brothels).

Furthermore, from this setup, the cover-up police actions reflect those of entrapment.

The defamatory damage, including perjury, was widespread, allowing me to use the police agenda to prove defamation after filing a defamation claim against my uncle and the police forces in 2021. I hoped this civil application would stop the cover-up. It did not. Anderson's lawyers, in Adelaide, SA, were in 2021 unwilling to take on the substantial case, a decision that clearly reveals their stance on the justice ladder. I knew this defamatory agenda, to which my fucked in the head uncle, the Labor government, and a paedophile police force-driven cover-up agenda could be proven. Technically, 'defamation' is distinct from perjury, with courts, media, and police forces applying defamation as a civil claim, whereas perjury is a criminal charge.

Utilising what had already been exploited, I used revenge porn to rebel against the narrative, continuing my crusade to prove defamation while using OnlyFans to personally investigate the excessive damages caused to my personal reputation over the past decade. I made it clear who I was, what I was sharing, and why, in talking video content for OnlyFans. No one had any reason to believe they should or could engage in solicitation and attempt to physically interact with me, a widely accepted professional among professionals now, for less than a few years, sharing content exploited by police forces, felons, and domestic violence, plus some new professional and unprofessional explicit content on the OnlyFans website. The space created a safe opportunity to capitalise on damages while protesting the narrative. Counteractive measures against defamation, ranging from financial losses for Barbwire Noose® to covering counteraction costs with this counteraction. OnlyFans earnings were used to fund Human Rights billboards and promote the initiative 'A Better World' globally. The platform has been empowering, viable, expressive, and a progressive step towards legal resolutions, even though my OnlyFans page was maliciously targeted, not even a year into being established, by unjustifiable activities.

It is irrefutable that law enforcement in Australia and abroad were on an entrapment mission to give cause to overlook government sex crimes in Australia and the circulation of revenge porn by Australian felons via the dark web – Silk Road. I am the most experienced whistle-blower in Australia – a notable achievement among government-employed officials across numerous advocacy sectors. Governance with little to no integrity. That big that almost every politician in government knows my name, with the media cowering in silence as events of torts, torture, and psychological warfare unfolded in a seedy cover-up of elite and police associated sex crimes.

Police forces collecting explicit and personal content from boyfriends and relations over the years had spread much R-rated content, amongst many circles of society. Yet, when I shared the same or equivalent content via OnlyFans, my account was met with interference from the CIA or FBI, and I was falsely accused of breaching policies, which was far from the truth. Travis Paul Enmon Jr. (DOB: January 16, 1989), my ex-fiancé, implies that the government did not like me earning money that they were not a party to. Which made no sense, as you provide your Australian Business Number (ABN) to earn funds, and these are declared at tax time via ABN.

The circulation of revenge porn via the dark web Silk Road, earning revenue without my consent, knowledge, or input, for years around 2012 and beyond, was fine for felons and the government to profit from, while the CIA and FBI, who shut Silk Road down, were privy to it. WTF is that if not one extraordinarily unjust and reckless exploitation of my being?

"If a nation expects to be ignorant & free, in a state of civilisation, it expects what never was & never will be. The functionaries of every government have propensities to command at will the liberty & property of their constituents. There is no safe deposit for these but with the people themselves; nor can they be safe with them without information. Where the press is free and every man able to read, all is safe." — Thomas Jefferson, The Papers of Thomas Jefferson, Retirement Series, Volume 9: 1 September 1815 to 30 April 1816.

The damage of perjury was everywhere as I travelled. Whether it involved international or non-international activity, the evidence of law enforcement's involvement in entrapment is irrefutable. I was able to use revenge porn to rebel against the narrative until SAPOL lied to USA law enforcement in hopes of getting the FBI on their entrapment train. They nearly achieved this, intelligence departments lacking intelligence and integrity, as I witnessed it, for the AFP, let alone the FBI, to focus on me and not paedophilia sex crimes, and the bikers peddling child porn was an abomination and not brave at all. Rebellious, I continued my crusade to prove perjury by law enforcement in a cover-up—an extraordinary chain of events stemming from SAPOL. The chain of causation to this perjury always leads to SAPOL – Kurt Slaven. I was able to personally investigate the excessive damage caused to my personal reputation over a decade. The fact that people I was friends with at school, people who knew my moral high-ground attitude and watched me study to qualify for a legal degree at university, could be convinced of malicious accusations with no basis or facts, was irrefutable proof of the severity of damages created by perjury in this desperate plot to cover up governance sex crimes. Authoring this series of publications, as well as two Royal Commission bombshell submission autobiographies before 2025, and nearing ten public disclosures in case I died books over approximately half as many years. I have made numerous autobiographical publications available for free download via the National Library of Australia, and they have been unchallenged regarding factual content since 2022.

Quoting world-renowned Author George Orwell, 1984 book Chapter 7 "If there is hope, wrote Winston, it lies in the proles - But the proles, if only they could somehow become conscious of their own strength, we would have no need to conspire."

The practice of governments distorting truths is not a new phenomenon. In my experience, no level of illicit engagement was off the cards, with attempts to distort the truth at times arising from blatant logical fallacies. You cannot turn irrefutable facts into assumptions. Trying to replace witness accounts and irrefutable evidence with maladministration is unlikely to conceal criminal negligence or a cover-up in this day and age. False documents are being used as a defence to sexual crimes, like the fanciful map drawn for the sell-out High Courts of Australia, which let George Pell (Catholic Cardinal) out of prison despite his crimes being overlooked and engaging in paedophilia. A High Court panel loyal to the government that appoints them is one of the reasons behind the erosion of Australia's constitutional law. These powers should always be separate.

For me, I shut down that type of malicious maladministration if I were confronted with this confusing and conflated agenda by presenting facts, photos, and supporting evidence in these books.

Upon release from Dame Phyllis Frost Centre, Victoria, AUS (VICPOL) 2022, the lying under oath by law enforcement and counterparts had circulated beyond extraordinary emergency circumstances. A two-decade-long plot to seed malicious accusations with no basis or facts of sex industry work upon my life had reached an irreparable, damaging level. VICPOL claimed the process I was enduring; severe reckless endangerment and a cover-up were the punishment for crimes I have never committed.

Tyrannical and unconstitutional laws had paved the way for sex offending to flourish in Australia under a totalitarian police force, despite my personal efforts to get on with life and attempts to counteract the perjury and defamation implemented for political gains. The perjury committed by SAPOL, in particular by Dave Kyriacou (SAPOL ID 40657), who wrote two false statements (perjury) chasing entrapment as a freemason, has resulted in damages that are beyond my ability to repair without resolution, public accountability, and compensation to the POLICE VS Kurt Slaven statement. By 2024, I saw Dave Kyriacou (SAPOL ID

40657) as a monster, not a man. With severe mental health issues – PTSD or something like that can only explain the actions of a 'likable cop', who engaged in perjury and an entrapment pursuit, which resulted in grievous bodily harm and sexual harassment, he literally encouraged.

Damages have been proven literally in the evident decline of my life and personal status since I assisted the police force. Since Dave Kyriacou (SAPOL ID 40657) arrived in Mount Gambier, South Australia.

In 2024, the government attempted to recoup proceeds from their crimes by charging people to download "The Story Behind the Brand BARBWIRE NOOSE®," attaching astronomical profiteering costs to download and print the book in an effort to deter readers, which, on some level, they likely achieved. The publisher also seemingly withheld payment of profits from the sales of The Story Behind the Brand BARBWIRE NOOSE® publication. Located in the United Kingdom, I rebelled against three tyrannical governments with Freemasonry at the core of their leadership, with years of victims calling out sex crimes in government, and leadership ignored by law enforcement across all three countries.

In 2025, the publisher of The Story Behind the Brand, BARBWIRE NOOSE, edition one, ceased printing, despite having received numerous orders and engaged in advertising expenditures months before this decision. A decision was made to release an unproofed edition by the publisher (with my loose approval), lacking even basic punctuation and grammar. Austin Macauley Publishers had one job and used any excuse not to do it, before the planned second edition of the book published in anticipation of NYFW and beyond, runway achievements.

The governance agenda, which at times involves desperately distorting truths, has been characterised by nitpicking formalities and attempting to make irrefutable facts assumptions through weaponised ambiguity and disinformation. This practice, which dates back to the 1950s, is a hallmark of MI6 and the CIA. Efforts of manslaughter and coerced suicide span back decades. Efforts to foil privacy breaches and Artificial Intelligence, the weapons of the elite, military, and law enforcement of modern times.

A cover-up is never okay or legal in governance. The nature of cover-up activities may constitute crimes such as Perjury, which is considered a crime in virtually all legal systems. Likewise, obstruction of justice, which is any activity aimed at covering up another crime, is itself a crime in many legal systems. The crime of making false statements (perjury), which includes not only providing misleading written statements, but it can also be verbal statements, extends to crimes of the withholding of information, entrapment, intentional and malicious activity, obstructions of justice, criminal negligence, duty of care, due diligence (not limited to these crimes/civil obligations) – the list of crimes surrounding cover ups goes on. Put that at the top of the Rebel 101 handbook, create unequivocal transparency. Plausible deniability is dead.

- 'Things taken and captured by pirates and robbers do not change their ownership.'

- 'What is first is truest and what comes first in time is best at law.'

These last two statements are Maxims of Law.

(Maxim – "a conclusion of reason"- Edward Coke, Coke on Littleton, 11a.) "A maxim is a proposition to be of all men confessed and granted without proof, argument, or discourse." Edward Coke. 67a. So-called…because its value is the highest and its authority the most reliable, and because it is accepted by all persons at the very highest. (William C. Anderson's A Dictionary of Law, (1893), page 666)

With reference to the *Little Engine That Could* which is an American folktale (existing in the form of several illustrated children's books and films) that became widely known in the United States after publication in 1930 by Platt & Munk. The story is used to teach children the importance of optimism and perseverance. The proof is in the pudding that these two values have been very much key to my legal and human rights successes.

I have been relentless with the police forces who recklessly endangered my life and have been criminally negligent. Refusing to be oppressed, to be ignored, or silenced. I have left messages on every police answering machine I could find, seeking a resolution. Years of emotionally distressed messages showing the level of extraordinary emergency, psychological warfare attacks, reckless endangerment, and criminal negligence committed against my person in a cover-up. Showing the levels of government invested in this cover-up and the endless amount of taxpayers' money that has been used to hide the truth. Leaving records endlessly within and externally through government departments and independently funded organisations. The facts are irrefutable, and the attitudes of the government employees involved in the cover-up are reminiscent of my experience at Sharley House. Everyone must have suspected Robert was sexually abusing these clients. Yet, Everyone had something to hide or cared more about protecting the taxpayer's income they received, rather than caring about the taxpayer who was their client. A client who relied on them for their welfare, as citizens rely on the police. A trove of employees willing to sacrifice lives for their easy, corrupt living. I witnessed callous chaos in disabled care and the police force. Two government-led departments have been plagued by employee demand issues – understaffed, underqualified, and an excuse to lower the standards of responsibility to criminally life-threatening levels. By 2024, I had heard and seen it all before.

Leaving endless records at times within and externally through government departments and independently funded organisations. I utilised recorded phone calls to government departments to expose malfeasance and criminality. Centrelink has that many recordings of the institutional abuses - illegal conduct from police forces desperate to distort the truth and refocus investigations in a cover-up of sex crimes. Sex crimes announced by me on their records and apparently gathered on record by law enforcement, also via my 'off' phone. Which is technically illegal as the police have no legal basis to investigate myself whose actions during a cover-up are protecting my life, my human rights, right to resolution and constitutional right to fair trial regarding the POLICE VS Kurt Slaven statement I made in 2017/2018, reported in 2014 and failing to meet trial in 2020 when SAPOL engaged in contempt of court ignoring a judge order to act on the evidence POLICE VS Kurt Slaven statement—this prolonged cover-up, myself at the whim of an extraordinary emergency.

Mentioning Centrelink, I will now discuss a rebellion by Aussies where the Australian government targeted low socio-demographic persons. Robodebt is just the tip of the iceberg regarding government welfare system abuses in Australia. Robodebt - ripping off the poorest in the country at this time, while the paedophile Hillsong church paid no tax. Seriously, the shamelessness of the government enslaving people who obey these corrupt policies for a job, I feel, is as much to blame as the government. If you see the government doing the wrong thing as an employee, you should be proud to say, 'No, I will not exploit my family, my neighbours, friends, and community.' Personally, I understand the costs to your livelihood if you speak out against the government, so I know why those who hold back do so. That being said, this should not be the way, and together we can change the practice of ostracism and dismissal as acceptable; we should. Heavily affected by the corruption of my fellow man, I also know the cost to a government worker and law enforcement members when they are involved in a cover-up – cover-ups are a crime; only power-tripping individuals think they are above the law. Those petty disruptions to welfare, institutional maladministration, and malpractice between friends show a lack of empathy, which is borderline psychotic behaviour from these people. Put bluntly, pursuing persons involved in maladministration to effect income in turn creates the circumstance where a government official is engaging in actions to deprive one of their liberties – malicious, premeditated actions intended to cause harm or at least emotional distress (psychological warfare).

Actions involving malicious, premeditated, or intended harm to another person are criminal. On one level, it could be argued that the irrefutable engagement in such actions should lead to at least a psychological assessment of a person's suitability for government or their role in government. Furthermore, upon the excuse used that

"I was doing what I was told," those complicit in corruption without accountability (totalitarianism) should be booked into a mental asylum because they have not evolved beyond monkeys (Nazis). I have no idea how they function alone.

The facts that un-trialled perjury caused an extraordinary emergency, had me stalked by sex pests, sex offenders, and police globally, are an abomination. Perjury of the vilest heights, putting Australia's association laws on the global stage of tyrannical legislation, with the statutes irrefutably being implemented for political gain, as well as the use of these laws to be weaponised against a whistle-blower to cover up sex crimes, is diabolical. My rebellious fight for resolution is real, on record, and truly an extraordinary emergency of survival against government, police, and felons involved in paedophilia within the sex industry and beyond. UGLY HEROS The Price of Unlawful Enforcement goes into the gory details. Here I am, in the basics, trying to encourage, guide, and inspire anyone and everyone to rebel against tyranny and fight the good fight for their human and Constitutional Rights – no matter what. No man is so above the law that he can kill, dehumanise, or disguise his irrefutable crimes at the expense of victims or the innocent. The focus of the government on low socio-demographic individuals, associations, or disabled persons with a plot to push the refuge of suicide, or furthermore, is genocide. Genocide is an internationally recognised crime where acts are committed with the intent to destroy, in whole or in part, a national, ethnic, racial, or religious group. Whether it be a genocide on the religious cult of Freemasonry, disabled, or the poor by government, military personnel, militia, etc, genocide is a serious crime to be involved in—nazi warfare. Riccardo Bosi (DOB9MAR1960) of Australia One party, a militia political activist in Australia, who I think should be charged with inciting hate at least, with an astronomical amount of evidence online and within his community support, which targets religion. Australian media call this man a 'cooker' (conspiracy theorist). Quoting the headline of a media article, it reads - 'Tear the place down': Inside cookers' bizarre plan to run for NSW Parliament. Two of Australia's best-known "cookers" have revealed their unhinged plot to "collapse the entire system" in a wild video. - February 10, 2023 - 10:01 PM (news.com.au). Personally, as a freemason, I have been the target of the hate he incites in his followers regarding Freemasonry. The bloke is a joke; jail is probably too good for him, yet by Australian law, that is what inciting hate results in. As I move forward to a career in politics in my latter years, this bloke had better be out of politics because I will pursue a charge of inciting hate regarding Freemasonry (religion) upon him after the years of military personnel hate I have endured as a future political candidate and Australia's most prominent whistle-blower.

Never let small-minded individuals deter you from taking action. Rebel.

A civil revolution where we stand up against this tyrannical system is this rebellion. Protest the Overrule as brand Barbwire Noose® #protestgraff puts it. Naming the brave of this time in history Kevin Shipp is a hero, Kyle Seraphin is a hero, Edward Snowden is a hero, Julian Assange is a hero, John Chris Kiriakou is a hero, David McBride is a hero; I am a hero, and everyone who stands after us, who stood before us and that really stood with us (countless and unnamed) at detriment or no benefit– ALL Heros.

The Rebellion, a 101 of everything fun and forthwith during corruption. The things worth dying for in life are often Us vs. Them – People vs. Power. We ended slavery, we ended the war that leadership always starts, we the people – united in our causes change the world! Here is to A Better World.

Anything But Ordinary

1. Regional Book Tour, Victoria - Stopped at DPFC.   2. Aussie
Whistleblower Julian Assange.   3. Backstage EASA TVC.   4. Global
TV Series.   5. OnlyFans.   6. Netflix 'True Colours'.

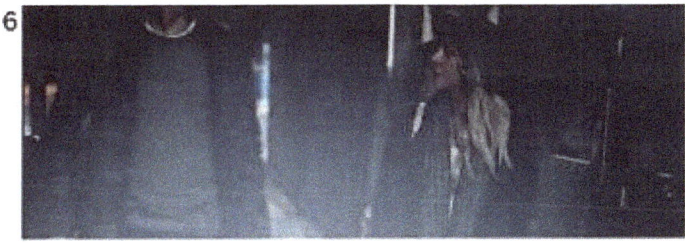

Chapter Two
'Fun Shit'

Live - Laugh - Love. Things I have done and enjoy doing!

Nothing beats a good road trip! Feeling alive driving at open road speeds, good music in the background, maybe a tinny with company you love. Having a yarn and a laugh, that is the makings of the best road trip.

Jumping out of a plane was fun. On the Mayan 'Last day of earth' 2012, I jumped out of a perfectly fine aeroplane with a cool guy named Fully. Sixteen feet, the best video where I look great, yet my behaviour is slightly Goober until we land on our feet - courtesy of my first timer self. The experience was absolutely EPIC! Check the jump out on Barbwire Noose YouTube if you want to see this in action!

Spontaneity is fun. A lot of my life's experiences have not been planned – for better or worse. I think that it is essential to live life to its fullest and to say yes to nearly every opportunity that presents itself to you. Even if you are a little uncomfortable doing it. Every moment you do not cease in life, you spend slowly doing nothing as you head towards the inevitable end of life. If I had said no as many times as I have said yes to life, I would have done very little. Instead of being jealous, be inspired. Embrace your inner God and be the best version of you possible, experiencing all the opportunities you are universally gifted.

Comedy is one of the most entertaining ways of spending time outside of live music, I think. I have had a great deal of fun at comedy gigs. Whether you attend a gig with friends or by yourself, the atmosphere of comedy shows is a blast. I have had the pleasure of spontaneously laughing my ass off at so many Comedians. Laughing my ass off too Ross Nobel (2022), Carl Baron during High School and since – the bloke is one funny guy, gold Logie winner Tom Gleeson (2023), you can catch anytime on the idiot box (2024)! The list of great comedians I've seen is numerous - whether broadly known or unknown, they are all funny. I attend every comedy gig I can, including numerous Melbourne International Comedy Festival and Sydney International Comedy Festival sideshows, as well as many local venues that feature comedians. I highly recommend getting involved in the fun of comedy if you haven't already. Break away from the Xbox, get off Netflix for a day, and leave the house - you can do it! I believe in you!

As a massive V8 supercar fan, I have had a great deal of fun in life so far, watching motor racing and even participating in promotional modelling at events. Nothing beats being behind the wheel of a V8, even if it is a Ford or a Mercedes—the sound, the smell, the grunt of three hundred kilowatts – a must-do mortal thing.

In love with Formula One and NASCAR, too, I am all in to drive these cars!

If you cannot ride a motorbike, learn. The great outdoors seems to be becoming a secondary pastime to technology these days, and boy, are people missing out. I grew up with a motorbike. Dirt motorbikes are so much fun and not as dangerous as you think (yet they are harmful – wear a helmet!). There are plenty of places to ride a motorbike safely. If you can ride a push bike, you can learn to ride a motorbike.

If motorbikes are not for you, Australia's outback offers plenty to enjoy, whether you hike, rock climb, cycle, swim, ski, hunt, or engage in a range of other outdoor activities.

Sitting at the football with a beverage, surrounded by fellow fans. Nothing beats live sport. I love cricket too! Matches are relatively low-cost if you have never been to a game. Put down the booze or something you could live without that costs for a month, and get yourself a ticket!

Just like drinking alcohol can be fun, marijuana can be fun too. Surprisingly, it is not fun when you're paying the government through the nose for flowers—just expensive seeds, grown under lights by someone with gloves and a hair net. Even though gloves and hair nets create unnecessary waste, street sellers were able to keep weed clean for decades without that shit. Marijuana, without the fun police government, is entertaining.

In 2023, on Earth Day, I found myself in the humble company of the Indian Sikh community. Getting involved with cultures, religions, and activities outside of your own community helps you grow and gain a deeper understanding of others. Though I have an Indian background, I knew little about the humble and brave Sikh community. Watching a celebration of the day and the Harvest period. Celebrations of tug of war, a three-legged race, potato sack races, and a dinner were provided. The experience was so much fun! I was able to plant a native shrub in the Olive Pink Botanic Gardens (Alice Springs, NT) to celebrate Earth Day, which was a significant experience. I found myself completely immersed in the family and community spirit, as well as outdoor games and the love for these community projects. I have been actively engaged with the Sikh community in Australia since 2023, and they are truly remarkable people. Culture is a wonderful experience, with all the different types of cultures, not just your own. The world would be a boring place without diversity.

I have travelled all over Australia. I do not necessarily remember all the names of the small towns I have visited, but I remember the people and the vibes of every region. We are truly a lucky country, and we need to protect this from our government's tyrannical ways. From Cobar, NSW, to Truro, South Australia, to

Tennant Creek, NT, to Chiltern, VIC, and beyond – I met many humble, helpful, and kind individuals who showed the Australian way. A way we all know and love – God bless this beautiful country and every character in it.

Chasing the Monitor lizard is a bit dangerous, yet fun. When I say 'chase,' I don't mean it literally; more like bird-watching, but it involves a lizard. These ancient creatures are stunning and elusive, fast and fierce, and definitely resemble the apparently extinct Australian Komodo Dragon, a gorgeous creature.

The best conversations I have had have been with randoms. Never underestimate the importance of being kind, slowing down in life, and engaging with a stranger in public (safely). Donate to the homeless, buy them a coffee, ask a local for directions – after all, they know their town best. Most importantly, take the time to listen to everyone with kindness and without judgment. This is where you learn and grow. Nothing is as precious as time, so always take time to do something other than your habitual daily grind.

Farm life. A country girl at heart, as history goes, and as my books bang on about. Seriously, country life is the best – I say never pass up the opportunity to spend time on a farm. Life and lifestyle take you back to what living is all about. Less device time in this day and age is always beneficial. Farm life is fun, proactive, active, and has an element of serenity and unpredictability that makes it unique. Even if you're a sheep farmer gearing up every morning for shearing, you never know when one of those sheep is going to lash out and kick you in the nuts! What fun. (Growing up next to sheep farmers, not smart animals they say!)

From hiking to rock climbing, camping under the stars with a fireplace to cook – being out in the wilderness is something my family always did. Whether it is canoeing, rock climbing, hiking, or absolutely roughing it, getting out into the great outdoors is liberating, invigorating, and rejuvenating. Walking in nature allows you to immerse yourself in the sights and scents of the world's flora and fauna. Personally, I have hiked in most states of Australia, camping in a few, and seriously, I would have to put a long walk on a mid-twenty-degree day through forests and over desert plains on my list of fun experiences.

Acting is fun, and anyone can be an Extra in a television show, movie, or advertisement! Seriously, anyone can give it a go, confident or not; you'll be surprised if this type of thing is for you. Being on set, you meet some really cool people! Then, after you have finished filming and been paid, it's a fun thing that keeps on giving excitement when you can watch your acting prowess and share these everlasting memories with family and friends.

Everyone is different, so my love for literature and fashion, which I have made careers out of, are not for everyone, but Squash is! Play it by yourself or with a friend, bashing that rubber ball against the wall with a racket is excellent for fitness and stress relief—fun times alone or with friends.

I never miss an opportunity to go go-karting. No matter what your age, get out there! Jumping on wheeled contraptions is fun. Man made the wheel, and suddenly we were mobile in more ways than one. What fun! Whether it was a homemade go-kart with a 125cc motor, a roll cage, and three gears (yes, I had one of these – Dad made it), or riding a fat-wheeled e-bike in the Australian desert (which felt rather fancy considering how rural I was!), travelling at speeds and cruising any terrain is a hoot. Petrol or solar charging, pedalling, or pushing—things with wheels are SiC! (SiC is a slang referring to something as Awesome, Great, etc).

Doing something new is living, and I often emphasise this. Reality is that life is short, and you are not here just to work and raise a family, as wonderful as these things can be. At least once a year, try something new and visit somewhere you haven't been before. Forget your age, throw caution to the wind, and enjoy living! God knows I do.

Eat different types of foods. Sounds lame, but I have had some of the most fun in my life eating at an expensive, well-rated, or well-catered restaurant. Whether you indulge in a single course and a drink or enjoy a seven-course designated menu, eating a gorgeous meal with the good company of others or yourself. Not needing to do the dishes and walking away feeling like you have had a real break from it all – that's fun.

Church is fun. Yes, you read that right. I go to church after a few spliffs (not always) in the morning and find my soul at peace in a space of kindness and love. Embracing God, any god, and understanding that the overwhelming things we do not know and cannot understand come from what we cannot understand, and that is God. That we were created out of love, and we are on this earth to strive and succeed as peaceful, productive beings.

Creating is fun and has propelled humanity forward through history. Make something, even if it has been made before. Create. Write, sing, dance – be creative, artistic. If your passion is digital creativity, pursue it! These things are not just great occupations, but also fun.

Celebrate your successes. Big or small. Alone or in a crowd, it is essential to acknowledge the good you do and rejoice in that positive energy. God knows, too many people focus on people's flaws rather than embracing positive behaviour.

Chapter Three
'Pieces of Australia' (through my eyes)

The list is long at times; all I can say is he was "A few stubbies short of a six-pack."

In 2023, I learnt the Zooper Dooper ice blocks were Australian. Here I was, nearly forty, thinking Vegemite was our biggest claim to fame in food.

FruChocs are a South Australian icon treat. If you don't know them, go into the supermarket and take a look. These Aussie gems, apricot-flavoured chocolate-covered balls, don't disappoint.

Nearly everywhere across Australia, you can find a 'Prince of Wales' and 'Crown and Anchor' pub. I am more of a toker than a tinny type. Yet, I do think Australian pubs are special. Grabbing the odd quick beverage at a local watering hole, you find friendly locals, underwear on the roof (possibly your grandma's), some freaky looking taxidermy (I'm sure Europe outdoes us here), rust (at times Lots of rust) and in a few places you'll find my Human Rights Activist name, brand Barbwire Noose® stickers or both.

The random kangaroo can be found anywhere throughout Australia. On the streets, in the outback, and on the dinner plate. Kangaroo tail is a delicacy that I have yet to try. As much as I have entertained the idea, I am keen to continue to avoid eating our giant hopping road hazards' tail, as much as one of my sisters (from another mister) says I am going to. Kangaroos will jump out in front of your car at any time in the Australian outback, especially at dusk, during sunrise, or after dark.

The Holden motorcar has defined Australia for decades. The iconic vehicles have represented our bogan culture and housed countless drug hauls since the seventies. They have driven our families across paddocks to school on a groggy school drop-off. Those bucket and bench seats were where your mamma conceived you and showcased your dad at his finest. The old, brown vinyl seats, cracking to pinch at the thigh, make a ride in an old Kingswood unforgettable. An authentic piece of Australian history is the forever-reliable ride in a Commodore.

In 2023, I visited Australia's only Organic (at this time uncertified) date farm during my Human Rights activism in the Northern Territory. Focusing on the positive in this moment before we head into the dangers of the outback, need I mention Ivan Robert Marko Milat (27 December 1944 – 27 October 2019) to express the possibilities of isolation. This farm was an Aussie experience. The Tamara Date Farm is an Oasis in the Desert. I actually never knew that a date was a product of a date tree. Believing it was something that derived from a plum tree. Discovering at thirty-nine years of age that the date tree is a palm-like plant and dates grow in large bunches, resembling giant grapes on the plant. It was a unique experience to see the farm's operation and beauty in such a barren place, situated in the middle of Australia's Northern Territory desert. Channel Ten's MasterChef stars Poh Ling Yeow and Adam Liaw had just visited and filmed at the farm, acquiring some dates, to cook a sticky date pudding, staff stated, for their SBS food channel telecast.

Such a beautiful backdrop! My first visit to the farm saw me sleeping in a tent under a clear night sky and witnessing an early morning meteor shower, as much as I wanted to see the meteorite shower, nights in the Northern Territory are freezing, so the only time anyone saw me this early morning was on OnlyFans, inside the tent! I actually hate tent camping; I'd rather camp with air conditioning in the car that took me to Whoop, Whoop, or with the luxury of a van, camper trailer, or caravan.

NOTE: I would not recommend visiting this farm—here's why… The farm, known for its quirks and perks among those familiar with it, offered a mix of pleasant and unpleasant experiences in its uncooperative yet cooperative environment. The place deemed unfit for WWOOFers (Worldwide Opportunities on Organic Farms) is a grassroots organisation that has been pairing volunteers with host farms since 1971. And rightly so, the accommodation, food, sexual harassment, and human rights violations volunteers are subjected to are understated (not understated by me, I tell it brutally as it is in ABO books and in UGLY HEROS Autobiography).

To start with, as a volunteer, I enjoyed a cosy stay on the farm's private property, equipped with power, water, and, so to speak, a real roof. After being told I would be staying in a tent, I complained, so I was given a space that matched what I had been promised. Lucky to be provided with a space with power and a heater, as I was promised before attempting the voluntary role at the property. While volunteering, I spent time on private property. Not the date farm. The date farm staff lied to volunteers to get them out to the rural location; they knew I personally required Wi-Fi and adequate space to study, work on my online fashion label, and write. Wi-Fi was not provided on the private property where I stayed during my visit. Luckily, I had a Starlink satellite connection for my online operations with Barbwire Noose® while travelling. The under-equipped volunteer quarters, which do not meet industry standards for accommodating volunteer roles, Kim McKay of the date farm said. Using the excuse that they were still under construction, though it was apparent that this was not the only lacking standard present. I appreciated Alan Thorp allowing me to stay on the powered and plumbed campgrounds – initially. After I sidestepped what I thought was a perfectly innocent invitation to the Finke event. The Finke Desert Race is an iconic annual off-road motorsport event featuring cars, buggies, trophy trucks, SXS, and bikes, held in Alice Springs. It seems Alan's attitude took a turn. Evidently, because I didn't want to be his next wife or whatever seedy plan he had for the trip to Finke.

For me, the experience was promised to be relaxing and productive. These were the volunteer conditions I was guaranteed to be stuck sixty kilometres outside of Alice Springs, without access to my car or a taxi to the property.

I was invited to the property under the pretence of a rest and relaxation (R&R) break, to interview and write about the farm's humanitarians (protesters, government rule rebels), and to share my life experiences for this book. Everyone was aware of this and very much encouraged my writing. I recognised that the farm was managed in a somewhat unusual way early on. The activities of the farm almost made me delete the paragraphs about them, as the truth about this desert Oasis is Ugly, and I wasn't sure I wanted to tarnish this book by talking about shit things, but it is interesting, so here goes.

I completely lost interest quite quickly in the alcohol fuelled, drug-use innuendo, which led to egotistic points of view being shared with me, not facts. I like facts. These autobiographies are facts, and I was surrounded by delusion. Accusations that my brand, Barbwire Noose®, displayed Nazi symbols, CPTSD triggers thrown about at the property, perjury that I was an informant, prostitute, and making porn for years. Old Gypsy Jokers' perjury was thrown around as fact, while old men fed alcohol and acid to teenagers and ogled teenagers in their care.

NOTE: In 2011, at the BMX Victoria and South Australia Country Championship, in front of my Mum, such vulgar and malicious defamation about porn was thrown about. It clearly started here, when Luke Hubert Scheidl (paedophile and Gypsy Joker) was peddling private videos (revenge porn) illegally and making some profits from the revenge porn that I did not know about. Freaks jumping on a freak's bandwagon. Seeing the operations of the date farm, I was not surprised. Luke Hubert Scheidl (paedophile and Gypsy Joker), with a creepy chick in Mt Gambier, who moved to Queensland, producing substandard porn for years, I learned in 2010. This chick is a loser who, for years, was jealous of my boob size in the local pubs and clubs of Mount Gambier whenever we would meet. In my eyes, Helen had been nasty to my best friend at the time, Christina, when they were working together as hairdressers. I never had any time for her and did flaunt my physique in her face – technically, my physique was on display for everyone, this was after midnight in a nightclub, not at nine am at church. The envious loser getting a boob job around this time (2009), funded partly by Luke Hubert Scheidl (paedophile and Gypsy Joker), before we met. The aspirations of some people to fuck old men and create creepy porn are not for me, but she consented. Not having given my consent to this activity myself, I did not suspect it would happen to me.

The rhetoric at the date farm, matching a decade-old defamatory claim, I had brushed off in 2011, didn't seem to be a coincidence, considering the seedy activity of the farm to me.

The drugs used on Tamara date farm weekly were stiff, heavy, and illicit. As the conversation spiralled out of control, so did the behaviour of the date farm staff. I was concerned for my welfare, especially as all members were making sexual advances (sexual harassment). The farm is a disgrace, running ten-year-old rhetoric (perjury), harassing women, fraternising with teens, dealing them drugs as fifty-year-old men claiming to be guardian-like figures. For me, the fucked-up behaviour aimed at me came as the Disability Royal Commission closed.

To make matters worse for me, the private property I was staying on was owned by a man said to be part of the seedy Freemason clique in the Northern Territory, and those close to him expressed that he had been asking me out on a date, not to watch the Finke event. I had been subtly propositioned to engage in casual sexual relations by numerous cooperative members of this farm, which was unwelcome, and I had made it very clear that I was coming out of an engagement to Travis Paul Enmon of the United States, after weeks of relentless efforts to engage with me sexually.

Sexual harassment, as I was a volunteer, the stay became awkward. Politely rejecting advances, I found myself fighting an inner urge to tell one particular resident of the farm, named Lorenzo (Enso) Mansori from Melbourne (Victoria, AUS), to "Fuck Off.". Enso was previously charged with raping an intoxicated woman in Victoria (VICPOL) and was acquitted of the charge, even though it is clear from his communication and having drunk with the man that he committed the sex crime. In the end, I did tell this felon to 'fuck off' amongst numerous other choice words in communication. In 2024, I received this threat from Lorenzo (Enso) Mansori via social media and website contact forms – 02APR2024, Message Details:

Name: Enso

Message: A FRIENDLY WARNING ⚠

MARCIA, YOU NEED TO REMOVE MY NAME OUT OF YOUR ARTICLE FROM THE DATE FARM. I HAVE SPOKEN TO MY LAWYER AND YOU HAVE BREACHED THE DEFAMATION IN CIVIL LAW. YOU MUST TAKE MY NAME DOWN NOW OUT OF THE DATE FARM ARTICLE OTHERWISE I WILL FOLLOW THIS UP FURTHER. ENSO

Email: *******@gmail.com

Subject: ARTICLE

A message to which I ignored for over a month until I replied with a 'bring it on' attitude, extracting the contents of this public disclosure for him to take to his sex offender protecting 'bullshit' lawyer. He went away, as the Truth is not defamation.

After a month of volunteering at the Date Farm, my CPTSD had been triggered at least a dozen times. Invited to indulge in the freedom of the land, the stay was barely relaxing. I was so uncomfortable that I timed the walk from the private property I was staying on, to the farm gate entrance in case I needed to call a taxi to pick me up and take me to my car, not that this was really an option as the cab wasn't keen to drive out to the date farm, it seemed. Being located so remotely and feeling unsafe, I had put Barbwire Noose® online via its own SpaceX, Starlink satellite instead of being dependent on the fickleness of members running the Tamara Date Farm. I knew little about cooperative operations. After this experience, I learned that a cooperative is somewhat similar to socialism, but not identical to it. By definition, a "Co-op" usually refers to a multi-work term agreement with one employer; in Australia, a co-operative is a member-owned business structure with at least five members. Co-ops are traditionally full-time, paid positions. An organisation, business, store, or farm that is owned and managed by a group of people who also work in it.

This farm was calling itself a not-for-profit and a co-operative, but members complained that they were not getting paid, and volunteering out there under these felons should have been completely stopped. The location is remote, and people are vulnerable to harassment and deprivation of liberties.

The Tamara Date farm was barely a business, the place was like a yearlong street party - you hang with your neighbours, bitch to and about your neighbours, if the click doesn't like new ideas, the tall guy living in number one, or the woman across the road won't fuck every single man on the street narcissism sets in, and people end up disliking each other. If the neighbour suddenly decides they are not cooking the arranged dinner tonight, you're too far out of the way to drive five minutes to Hungry Jack's (Burger King) for food.

The farm ran on at least one regular, weekly trip to Alice Springs (NT, AUS) to obtain supplies, and during harvest, possibly twice a week to post-date box orders.

The Tamara date farm has relied on the generosity of volunteers to survive in its operations for years, they told me. God knows why you would treat volunteers so poorly – women, at least. They are best off sticking to milking their friends and family, if you ask me; it beats getting sued by people like me, which I have expressly stated that I planned to do regarding defamation and perjury. The full-time working members, desperate for cash they expressed this during my stay. Desperation that I witnessed turned into harassment when Enso and his 'boss', Denis (cooperative member), as Enso referred to him, took the path of planning to gain drug sales opportunities and protection from the police by embracing the affray of defamatory remarks and perjury that had caused damages and grievous bodily harm offences against me for years. These lost from reality people calling me crazy – like false statements written by SAPOL police to cover up paedophilia, the defamatory claims from members also stating that I had been a prostitute, like both SAPOL and NTPOL police who were involved in ICE (methamphetamines) and the sex industry, on top of the Nazi accusations about my more Freemason-oriented than anything else brand.

This unique piece of Australia is a historical fuck up. Still, I am sure it would be worth visiting after the sex offenders, drug abusers, and potential violence against women offenders are removed from the farm. An experience with volunteer work that suits all ages and is within your realm of opportunity, provided the environment is made safe. A beautiful piece of Australia that deserves to be untarnished by sex offenders hiding in the desert.

Indigenous cultures and people, the native Australians, are fascinating, with a fantastic culture and community practices that look after the country, preserve bloodlines, avoid disabilities, and incorporate traditional stories that connect the stars and the sky with everyday life—an invaluable part of the Australian continent's history.

Anything But Ordinary

Australia is known for its distinctive bogan lingo, casual and laid-back attitudes, and stunning landscapes. To me, what makes Australia great is our freedom, our Indigenous peoples, and our commitment to protecting the environment, which should be respected and valued. Over the 2023/2024 period, the government allowed an influx of immigration from countries known for their pollution and substandard conditions, which is seriously disheartening. Homelessness, discussed in 2021 in politics, increased to the point where Aussies lived in tents by 2024, while the government funded immigrants to take jobs, as others travelled across the country like I did. These immigrants are destroying the countryside with rubbish, as I witnessed personally.

Mining in Australia has both enriched and impoverished the country, affecting the health of many citizens and damaging a significant portion of the environment. It's a profitable stain on much Indigenous land, and it takes a specific type of person to make a career out of mining, I think, like most professions. Those who stay long-term are a type. Certainly not my type. The fly-in, fly-out lifestyle of West Coast of Australia employees is not something I find interesting or enviable. Yet it is worth noting that the mining industry provided many jobs for my peers and Australians in general at this time, which I support. What I don't support is mining pollution and pillaging land, so it looks like Coober Pedy, South Australia. Mining has ruined the landscape there.

Adding to this culture, lacking environmental care, is infidelity.

Personally, I endured some creep with a family from STARForce SAPOL (Darren Walker) in 2018, who crept around me as I flew to EFWA2018, talking about how he was friends with the 'Vogue' Magazine writers, and tried to extort this opportunity for Barbwire Noose to be featured in the magazine as my brand graced the runway for the second year running. I was not complicit in his pursuit, so Barbwire Noose® did not feature with 'Vogue' this year. Which he implied was an opportunity if I complied. I don't conform with seedy creeps, nor does Barbwire Noose® – 'Do NOT Conform'. This is the 'type' in mining I'm talking about. Seedy meetings on planes, doing whatever in and out of relationships, not only shows the immorality of the industry, which spills over into how they pillage the land, but furthermore solidifies the unsavoury background connections these industries have with sex industry associated sidekicks, stemming into government benefits. Australia's political climate is exposed as an alcohol indulgent rape fest; if one can get away with alcoholism or seedy ongoings, they will. Like the Liberals, Bruce Lehrmann (Born in College Station, Texas, in June 1995) grew up in Toowoomba, QLD, and was involved in a cover-up scandal surrounding his raping of his co-worker, Brittany Higgins, in Parliament House. Money corrupts—

bullshit funding bullshit, associated with bullshit as seen through my eyes.

Ending this chapter on Australia with something every Aussie should agree on, nothing beats our beaches! We have some of the most beautiful coastlines in the world, and although I haven't seen the whole world, I have seen most of Australia's coastlines. Our waters are pristine, and our sands shimmer in the sunshine. You cannot beat Port MacDonnell, South Australian crayfish, nor the fish and chips from this coastline. I grew up in this wonderful region, and travelling all over Australia, I've heard the same from many who visit the Crayfish capital. If you visit Australia, make sure you grab yourself a six pack of your favourite drink, dig a hole in the sand to where it's cool and wet - if you don't have an Eski, chuck your drinks in the hole to keep them cool, get yourself the best fish and chips around down South Australia and enjoy your time on the coast.

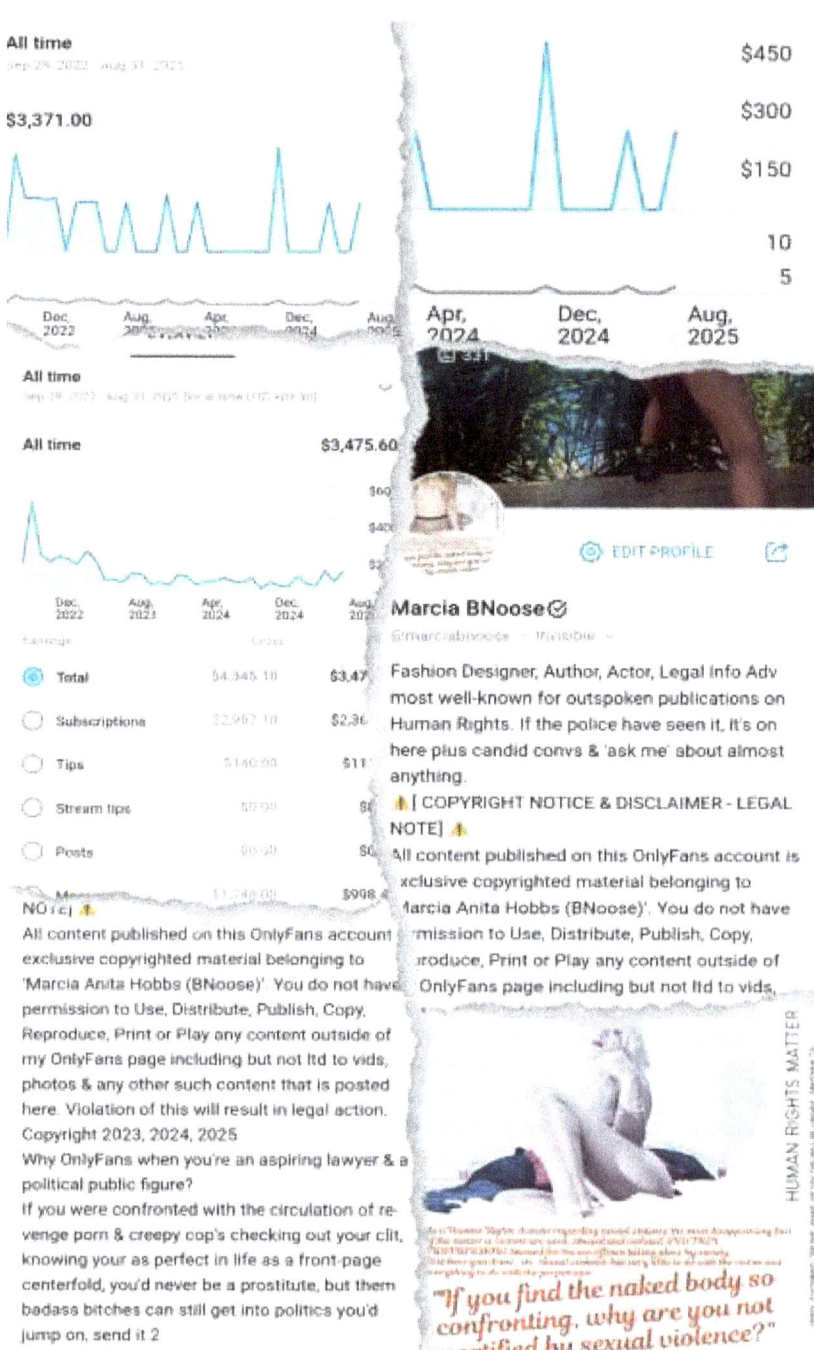

All time
Sep 29 2022 - Aug 31 2025

$3,371.00

$450
$300
$150
10
5

Dec, 2022   Aug, 2023   Apr, 2024   Dec, 2024   Aug 2025

Apr, 2024   Dec, 2024   Aug, 2025

All time
Sep 29 2022 - Aug 31 2025 (local time UTC +09:00)

All time $3,475.60

$60
$40
$2

Dec, 2022   Aug, 2023   Apr, 2024   Dec, 2024   Aug 202

Total	$4,345.10	$3,47
Subscriptions	$2,967.10	$2,36
Tips	$140.00	$11
Stream tips	$0.00	$
Posts	$0.00	$0
Messages	$1,248.00	$998

EDIT PROFILE

Marcia BNoose ⊘
@marciabnoose · Invisible

Fashion Designer, Author, Actor, Legal Info Adv most well-known for outspoken publications on Human Rights. If the police have seen it, it's on here plus candid convs & 'ask me' about almost anything.

⚠️ [COPYRIGHT NOTICE & DISCLAIMER - LEGAL NOTE] ⚠️

Why OnlyFans when you're an aspiring lawyer & a political public figure?
If you were confronted with the circulation of re-venge porn & creepy cop's checking out your clit, knowing your as perfect in life as a front-page centerfold, you'd never be a prostitute, but them badass bitches can still get into politics you'd jump on, send it 2

📍 Australia

HUMAN RIGHTS MATTER

"If you find the naked body so confronting, why are you not mortified by sexual violence?"

Chapter Four

'Pieces of Me'

Always remember that the evil Wants You to dwell on your mistakes. – Marcia Anita Hobbs, Lodge 406.

Things you may know or may not know about me are that, despite authoring three autobiographies, which are tell-alls, plus this series, once upon a time, my aspirations to join the Australian Army were Real, not about book writing or fashion designing. Yes, that's right! Little princess wanted to be on the frontline and shoot at the enemy from the dugouts. After growing up on a farm and playing army with my brother, I downloaded basically the entire army website and printed it off, ready to become a soldier. However, I soon realised two things: one, I couldn't be a frontline soldier in 1999, and two, Dad wouldn't let me join. This occupational desire is mentioned in UGLY HEROS: The Price of Unlawful Enforcement. The details are that I practised and passed the required physical push-ups and sit-ups, and I also practised the necessary running. I was in year eleven at school. My Uncle, who had actually been in the Army, got in the ear of my father, stopping this career interest due to the Army not being a place for women. Heavy sexual abuse numbers to which my uncle was aware due to his personal army service, coupled with my will to play with guns as a front liner, the role was not open to girls, so I took the good advice that was given and explored psychology, and veterinary practice to pursue my passion for law, finally. Admittedly, as an adult, I am not a fan of camping, so the Army would have sucked.

I lived out of home for over fifteen years before I had to do my own dishes and take out my own bin. I wasn't really pleased that life had reached the point where I had to do these chores myself. Chores, I'll add that were short-lived. While single, I decided it was best to live off of take-out, pizza, boiled eggs, and paper plates and wooden cutlery. Proud adulting right here.

At the age of thirty-eight, I learnt how to properly fold a fitted sheet, even though the laundry is my thing—gone are the days when I fold that thing in half, then half again, and then in half again - maybe—scrunching it into a Square mainly by just tucking the sides into the folds and settling with it, looking like a square! Yay me.

Not all my teeth are real. I have had a crown implant since my early twenties. An implant crown is an artificial tooth that is fixed to the jaw or cheekbone, which gives it the strength and durability of a regular tooth. Once fitted, an implant crown connects to the bone through a process called osseointegration, whereby new bone cells grow around the screw-like "post" and keep the crown secure. I had four wisdom teeth removed when the screw plate was fixed into my jaw, and I took zero painkillers after this dental surgery.

My favourite colours (shades) are pink and black. Colours which played a predominant part in Barbwire Noose BN Couture designs for the debut Eco Fashion Week Australia runway of 2017.

My pet peeve is sheep behaviour. Someone who unthinkingly follows a clearly misguided crowd out of ignorance and greed is a societal burden—no Sheeple zone.

I've been skinny dipping in the remote outback, near Kings Canyon, NT, and run up the side of Ayers Rock (Uluru), despite the government trying to tell people they can't climb it, as they claim it damages the rock, as well as its First Nations significance. I have visited Uluru (Ayers Rock) numerous times; it is a beautiful, natural wonder.

People who nitpick words are annoying. If your argument and/or justification is that you're resorting to grammatical references or picking words to find offensive, save us both time and shut up. I don't care for grammar Nazis, especially those ignoring facts for a petty argument.

I have worked in government roles since I was 16 years old. Knowledge is power, they say; evidently, this is so." Sometimes I should have just gone straight to university; other days, I think about what wouldn't have changed if my path hadn't been the same.

Featured on the runway of Eco Fashion Week Australia 2018 was a design I had planned to wear as a feature on my wedding day (ruined, as the choreographer's daughter held up the train, even though she looked lovely; it did the dress an injustice). This dress was planned to be a feature at my wedding to Travis Paul Enmon Jr. (born January 16, 1989), until 2022, when I no longer wanted to marry him. In October 2020, SAPOL, via a property owned by Vivienne Dunstan, stole this one off an Organic 'BN Couture' dress tailored to my physique design, so this may have ruined the opportunity before Travis did.

The qualification I was accepted to study in 2001 (deferred until 2002) at Flinders University, Adelaide, SA, was Justice and Society—a step into what would have led me to study criminal law.

I am just over five feet tall and have never weighed more than sixty kilograms, averaging around fifty kilograms for my entire adult life.

I am a dog person, but I also like cats. Prefer dogs – not a massively important fact (saves the direct messages replies!)

I do not reply to stupid questions in my direct messages. Random messages, maybe, "what's your favourite pet?" questions you can get answers about in these books, and you never know – I could actually change my mind with age.

Anything But Ordinary

Numerous times, I've nearly died – some of these events are detailed in ABO book 1, while others have not yet occurred. From a pole coming at my head in a car accident, nearly being squashed by a building accident, snake encounters, falling off motorbikes as a child, a flying gnome almost hit my head as a child, a machete wielding nut job, strangulation in domestic violence, an attack with a knife by a bloke I wouldn't marry, a plot to overdose myself during sex with drugs inserted in my anus; these are the most prominent and significant near death experiences I've had.

I fast on most Sundays, practising discipline and gratitude. The practice taken up in my thirties has been quite enlightening. Not for reasons you would think. And no God has not appeared because I starved for him. Fools have appeared instead. Some try to feed me on this day, while others talk about food or put it in your face. The practice has literally exposed the quality of the people around me. Remember, these types of actions are disrespectful. Not only does fasting teach discipline and gratitude, but it also reveals who your genuine friends are, apparently. It's not that tosser who's talking about how he ate in your face while you fasted, that is for sure.

I wake up early and am very talkative. I am absolutely a morning person (no need to dm's that question either!).

I go to bed early unless it's a party or there is something to do. I don't often stay awake to watch TV unless I'm with company.

I'd rather put a movie on timer and watch it in bed, knowing I'm likely to lose interest as sleep is more important to me than TV.

Quote: "If she'd done something, she'd be on TV!?" - Serious, shit I hear from Family—the 'she' clearly me. And fame apparently the bar whistleblowing is aiming for (WTF) - clearly being on TV like 'normal people' for a bit of acting matters not. A public figure, fame is not a definition I strive for. Family literally ignored facts to (like the police ignore sex crimes in a cover-up – the side you're on is obvious!!). I was chosen for NYFW designer operations, interviewed on an American podcast for whistleblowing, and have numerous global books featuring autobiographical and public information disclosure, among many other books and professional media appearances.

At this time, my head was on Netflix (2023) -'True Colours', which was only sitting around number one most watched in Australia. But hey, ignore me and the obvious, as well as my day-to-day activities, like my activism; you can't really ignore that, but people do. My family is an unbelievable source of envy.

Barbwire Noose® threads have been advertised on billboards globally for years, with BN Couture designs sold in New York City, USA - let's ignore the facts, though. Always fun. I also appeared in the SBS series and numerous TVCs, including one in the NT, which was aired in 2022, just before the family made this comment in 2023.

Protest broadcast on NITV in 2021, Channel 9 and Channel 7 in 2024, etc. Not that I actually advertise my achievements at family gatherings, but since I've been the flavour of the month via my social media posts and gossip, here's keeping you all up to date...

...technically, I've been on TV since I was eight (or something like that) years old. I am often featured in newspapers and magazines, and have numerous books that showcase my achievements, which some of my family members have copies of. Still, they ignore those facts to (like the police ignore sex crimes in a cover-up – the side you're on is obvious!!). I was chosen for NYFW designer operations, interviewed on an American podcast for whistleblowing, and have numerous global books featuring autobiographical and public information disclosure, among many other books and professional media appearances.

But hey, I have definitely achieved nothing – said, rolling my eyes into the back of my head. Keep judging me as an underachiever. Why don't you? More importantly, talking about someone you barely know, because you have nothing better to do with your clearly busy lives, looks good on you. Sarcasm flowing through the roof here. My God, I despise jealousy – just be happy for people – Stop Hatin'.

My current favourite movies are Marvel and DC series, such as Wonder Woman, Captain America, and Thor. The 'Sound of Freedom' CIA investigation-based movie made me cry; unfortunately, I couldn't watch that twenty times – great movie though. Seeing the iconic Barbie at the cinema, cinemas are a great place to unwind. Sitting at home with Netflix and paid movies is okay, but nothing beats the big screen and laughing, crying, sighing along with peers you know and don't know.

These are just some 'pieces of me'.

Chapter Five

'History'

"Those who cannot remember the past are condemned to repeat it." – George Santayana, The Life of Reason (1905) from the series Great Ideas of Western Man.

Which is EXACTLY what some historical accounts want.

I study a great deal of war history; my opinions in this book are based on facts and also offer my perspective on modern developments. Always conduct your own research from multiple sources. The best accounts of history come from people who lived through the times and from what has physically manifested, allowing you to see, touch, or feel it. Disinformation is everywhere, propaganda is a weapon, and the truth is hidden in plain sight.

At the time I was authoring this book, the lands of the Arrernte communities were bleeding from the loss of a teenage boy whose life was taken by an ex-military police officer of NTPOL. R.I.P. Brother.

"Again, were we to inquire by what law or authority you set up a claim [to our land], I answer, none! Your laws extend not into our country, nor ever did. You talk of the law of nature and the law of

nations, and they are both against you" - Lewis Corntassel, 1891
(Cherokee).

This incident was racially driven, radical, and unwarranted, yet even the lowest charge regarding the loss of this life was not implemented. White supremacy reigned in court, and now black supremacy reigns in the street as the unrest and divide of racial outcomes drives hate into the children who saw, heard, and felt their peers die without police accountability. Most say and would agree that if the person who was killed were white, the outcome would have been different. After spending much time with the Alice Springs (NT) community and witnessing racism firsthand in their police station, I agree.

Marijuana was legalised across Australia, and police forces were disrupting the delivery of the Therapeutic Goods Administration (TGA) approved medical Marijuana in shipments via airports and post offices—sad facts about the legalisation of a medicinal plant. The government, as I have seen it, was not serious about Australians using the plant medicinally over pharmaceutical alternatives, setting the price to purchase medicinal Marijuana at a level higher than street value averages across the Nation. Personally, I felt the full effects of the government in control of medicinal Marijuana as they disrupted the delivery of my CPTSD treatment in hopes of pushing me to the refuge of suicide before UGLY HEROS The Price of Unlawful Enforcement was corrected after Australia and USA law enforcement targeted a whistle-blower for the government to cover up sex crimes committed in Australia and clearly beyond our water's borders. The facts are that Australia was not the first to wage war on the love-spreading plant cannabis, and we certainly were not the first to plant it. Yet, we were the first caught using the legalisation as a bid to wage war on civilians. Cannabis was first said to arrive in Australia in the 1770s when hemp seeds were brought to Australia from the United Kingdom by Sir Joseph Banks aboard the First Fleet.

The First Fleet comprised 11 ships transporting convicts from Portsmouth, England, to New South Wales, the penal colony that would become the first European Settlement in the country.

Joseph Banks, an English naturalist and botanist, marked the hemp seeds as "for commerce," hoping that the plant would be produced commercially in the colony.

Historians believe that hemp cultivation was a primary motivation behind colonisation. According to Dr Jiggens, Australian historian and author of Sir Joseph Banks and the Question of Hemp, Britain's colonisation of New South Wales was never about finding a place to relocate convicts but to turn it into a hemp colony.

Hemp was of great importance to maritime countries, as it could be used to make cables, sails, and other valuable items. With Joseph Banks' help, cannabis was introduced in Australia, where it flourished and was widely used during the 19th century. The government encouraged hemp farming for the next 150 years by giving grants and land.

Cannabis was used for both recreational and medicinal purposes. Cigars de joy (cannabis cigarettes) were sold over the counter well into the 20th century in Australia. These are claimed to give immediate relief from asthma, shortness of breath, influenza, bronchitis, and cough-related ailments.

As I understand it, the Early 1900s were the First significant attempts at Prohibition.

Like most developed countries, the Australian cannabis prohibition journey began in the 1920s. This is when the domestic implementation of international drug control treaties set off the eventual cannabis prohibition in the Commonwealth.

The first attempt at banning cannabis was in the 1912 International Opium Convention. Luckily, the United States' attempt to include cannabis in the 1912 Convention signed at The Hague was unsuccessful.

The 1912 Convention's primary objective was to control exports and restrict opium, heroin, cocaine, and morphine to medical uses only. It didn't make drug use or cultivation illegal. Like others negotiated by the League of Nations, this Convention was normative rather than prohibitive.

This led to the United States and China, which favoured prohibitionist measures, withdrawing from negotiations that led to the 1925 International Opium Convention signed in Geneva.

1925 The Geneva Convention – Cannabis Prohibition in Australia, Cannabis banning was inevitable. A revised International Convention relating to Dangerous Drugs was signed at Geneva. A treaty designed to outlaw the recreational use of opium and cocaine. Egypt is making a last-minute request to include cannabis, as "it was causing widespread insanity." Turkey backed the motion, but India opposed it.

Cannabis has frequently been the object of unsound laws and discriminatory enforcement, and is increasingly being decriminalised or legalised globally, as with psychedelics such as psilocybin. Natural plant-derived medicines have been extensively academically researched regarding their potentially profound effects to treat mental health disorders.

It is also worth considering when evaluating the history of drug and alcohol policy, the place of addiction in discussions. Different understandings of addiction can yield very different perspectives on these policy debates.

One traditional view of addiction is a kind of moral failing. Unlike people who moderately use substances such as drugs or alcohol, the addicted person uses these substances immoderately -

seemingly without regard for the harm that they may cause to themselves or others. As a form of immorality, the view of addiction through a moral lens, if one thinks of addiction this way, makes prohibition seem like a natural policy measure. After all, one of the activities of the state is to prohibit and impose criminal sanctions on immoral behaviour. Labelling substance abuse as just another form of sinful behaviour, then it could seem to make sense to prohibit it. Nearly all experts now reject this moral model of addiction. Many psychologists favour a medical model of addiction, in which addiction is understood as a chronic disease. From this point of view, the prohibition of alcohol or other drugs can seem perverse. If drug or alcohol use is the symptom of a disease, then it seems senseless to prohibit it, just as much as it would be foolish to prohibit the symptoms of diabetes and other ailments or diseases.

Medical Marijuana legalisation is not enough to stop industrial control and government prevention to profit, the seed needs to be free. Free from chemical-based hydroponic medicinal production. The seed is ours, not the governments or industries; the seed is for the people and should be free as God intended it to be. Genesis 1:29 King James Version (KJV) And God said, Behold, I have given you every herb bearing seed, which is upon the face of all the earth, and every tree, in the which is the fruit of a tree yielding seed; to you it shall be for meat.

Japan's invasion and war with the USA at Pearl Harbour left the window open for the Japanese to infiltrate the USA through Hawaii. Despite a large USA Navy base in Hawaii, communication intel has been distorted for decades, and intelligence has seemingly been misled to the point where many information gathering networks have become so lazy that they believe any bullshit people put to them via privacy breaches – I have witnessed analytics intelligence manipulation firsthand. The whispering of your enemies is real. In Australia, China recently established a Consulate base in Adelaide, South Australia, while targeting the Uyghur community heavily here in our country, which I witnessed firsthand. The first thing China advertised on this Consulate website was its Japanese counterparts. The plight of the Asian century is still very much alive, as promised to China during the Nazi war, even though we are a quarter of the way into the rise of communism. History teaches us that the attack on Pearl Harbour was a surprise military strike by the Imperial Japanese Navy Air Service on the American naval base at Pearl Harbour in Honolulu, Hawaii, in the United States, just before 8:00 a.m. (local time) on Sunday, December 7, 1941. At the time, the United States was a neutral country in World War II. The attack on Hawaii and other U.S. territories led the United States to formally enter World War II on the side of the Allies the day following the attack, on December 8, 1941. The Japanese military leadership referred to the attack as the Hawaii Operation, Operation AI, and Operation Z during its planning.

The Empire of Japan's attack on Pearl Harbour was preceded by months of negotiations between the United States and Japan over the future of the Pacific. Japanese demands included that the United States end its sanctions against Japan, cease aiding China in the Second Sino-Japanese War, and allow Japan to access the resources of the Dutch East Indies. Anticipating a negative response, Japan sent out its naval attack groups in November 1941 just before receiving the Hull note—the United States' demand that Japan withdraw from China and French Indochina. Japan intended the attack as a preventive action. It aimed to prevent the United States Pacific Fleet from interfering with its planned military actions in Southeast Asia against overseas territories of the United Kingdom, the Netherlands, and the United States. Over the course of seven hours, Japan conducted coordinated attacks on the U.S.-held Philippines, Guam, and Wake Island, and on the British Empire in Malaya, Singapore, and Hong Kong.

Yet, through Hawaii, many Japanese immigrants have passed into the USA, with Hawaii adopting many Japanese traditions, which can be witnessed upon flying into and landing in this region of the USA. The Navy was what many claim Hitler used to peddle advanced military technology, including invisible technology, in 1940, as well as intelligence claims of escapes and other sinister and seedy forms of transportation. Navy combat is an isolated occupation. Studies have shown that the reintegration of veterans into civilian life presents a spectrum of challenges that can hinder their adjustment and well-being. One such challenge is cultural disconnection, where veterans may struggle to feel connected to civilian cultural norms and practices, making social integration particularly challenging.

Identity Crisis: Transitioning from a highly structured military identity to a civilian one can create an identity crisis for many veterans, complicating their sense of purpose and self-worth. Personally, I have been stalked, sexually assaulted, and targeted by psychological warfare by military men, particularly Navy personnel – all these men sharing a few commonalities: the purchasing of wives, self-isolation habits, sexual abuse, and identity crisis, including gay and transsexual tendencies. Knowing these as psychological factors, I wonder why history has not taught us to nurture the minds of men in these roles and to be less tolerant of post-war plots to invade countries through psychological and financial means when the war is lost on the battlefield. China vows to win the war on economic fronts, as with Nazi Germany. Until we recognise that wars are never really over in the minds of men, we will never really see peace. Australia's history of colonisation still stains our Indigenous culture, generations, and history to this day. Forgive and forget are not virtues - equality, mutual respect, and sovereignty are the ways a country can protect its peace and bring peace. Multicultural communities are wonderful, yet they are a dream of conflicting religions and standards living in harmony. Religion teaches hate as much as it teaches love, and it has very much been the drive of many wars amongst countries, not just the communist and democratic fights that underlie religion and power.

The New Order (German: Neuordnung) of Europe was the political and social system that Nazi Germany wanted to impose on the areas of Europe that it conquered and occupied.

Planning for the Neuordnung had already begun long before the start of World War II. Still, Adolf Hitler proclaimed a "European New Order" publicly on 30 January 1941: "The year 1941 will be, I am convinced, the historical year of a great European New Order!" Hitler's ideas about eastward expansion, which he promulgated in Mein Kampf, were greatly influenced during his 1924 imprisonment and his contact with his geopolitical mentor, Karl Haushofer. One of Haushofer's primary geopolitical concepts was the necessity for Germany to gain control of the Eurasian Heartland to attain eventual world domination. Also relevant was the idea that an alliance with Italy and Japan would further augment German strategic control of Eurasia, transforming those states into the naval arms protecting Germany's insular position. Nazi Germany and the Nationalist government of the Republic of China maintained bilateral relations between 1933 and 1941. The Chinese Nationalists sought German military and economic support to consolidate control over warlord factions and resist Japanese imperialism. The relationship between China and Japan is complex, yet Japan's rise in Western societies is as historical as the plan of the Asian century aligned with Nazi communism.

The Asian Century refers to the dominant role Asian nations aspire to play in the 21st century, driven by rapidly growing economies, military advancements, and population growth. The rise of China can only be understood in the context of the decline of free-world economics. This is a democracy vs. communism—more accurately, a dictatorship battle—and personally, I want democracy to win.

Chapter Six
'Making Music'

Hell and Sunshine, that's how you taste - Tantalising.

I wrote a love song for this guy once. He was so touched. All he heard was, I Love You. He gushed that no one had done this for him before.

I was shocked. I expected more.

Tears, heartbreak, and a small piece of the ache I had whispered.

With no microphone to do the recording justice, I had crafted a beat just for him.

Cool, calm, clueless.

Clueless, he was. For this song told him I could not marry him. It told him we were not meant to be, back in the Autumn of 2022. He did not hear me. He never did.

Between lust and immaturity. He never quite understood that I was the beginning of the end—the end of his lies and the beginning of something more.

I sat there, wide-eyed on the screen, basking in his ignorance. He was cute yet not at all innocent, in this moment and moments to follow.

As time passed and the months turned into a year. He still had not realised that I had told him long ago that I could not marry him. That we were over. That the sweet nothings he hears me whisper are sweet nothings of goodbye. That at this point I would only marry him if I were to die, for my love for the moon is never-ending, and an eclipse.

A song, my first song, that whispers to you, my love. Telling you I don't know how to tell you that I no longer do. Always my love.

For the fifty-zillionth time in my books, I'll say – I love music. Anyone who knows me knows this. In 2021, I decided to start experimenting with making some. There are some grouse apps to get your groove on about these days. However, there was nothing groovy about my compilations to start with. Mellow, with a bit of tech-type sounds. I was sending my music—we'll call them demo EPs—to my ex-fiancée, Travis Paul Enmon Jr. (DOB: January 16, 1989), who had no idea the music was mine to start with. A lead singer and guitarist who had dabbled in the American heavy metal scene, Travis was locked up in Berkeley County Detention Centre, South Carolina. He had been incarcerated for a year and still had many years to serve due to assaulting his mother and perjury, from what I could see. The Feds upgrading his charges in 2024 was, to me, an evidence-based reflection of his lies (perjury) versus the evidence. Perjury is the last thing anyone should resort to for leniency, especially when it involves victims. You could induce a charge of perjury by feigning innocence and intel, too, which is not beyond many. We were talking via an inmate video app, which could send message videos. I was admittedly contemplating whether we had a future or not, but the not won. He was not locked up when I agreed to marriage and had not committed the domestic violence offences which led to his incarceration when we verbally got engaged. He was around the fourth or fifth musician I had been involved with, from pub solo gig players to recording-level bands. I like music and musos, it seems.

Anyway, in the background of these music videos, I would put the music that I made up. Before Travis knew I was making the music, his comments were positive, as he thought I had acquired it from a professional source. This feedback was good to me, so I disclosed that the music was mine. That is when I sent him a short interlude-like song, just for him, which he missed the central message of. To busy trying to profit from the video while in jail without my consent. I had sent him money to buy extra needs and food in jail, and he was fat; he did not need to violate our privacy for cookies, but Travis is a try-hard. Always wanting to be the 'cool cat'. I could do nothing about the damage once it was done. So, I stopped sending him money, and then I stopped sending him videos after I got him back for his engagement in revenge porn and solicitation. Forgiving and forgetting are not on the cards when it comes to exes; I hold a grudge.

Since I was very young, I have loved to dance and sing. Dad bought me a red microphone, and I would sing in my room. At times, Dad would walk down the hallway past my bedroom and sing back to the lyrics. Bellowing things like "we know your name" as I sang the band Goo Goo Dolls' song Iris. I would make up lyrics in my head. Sing it out in a kind of rap way, imagining some basic beats in the background. Lyrics flow to me like poetry flows with me. Expressions via words, tones, sounds – verbalising a message is a natural talent.

Music the Muse. I was young when I started to dabble in songwriting. I would make up lyrics in my head and sing them out in a kind of rap style, imagining some basic beats in the background.

The side hustle has always been fashion before it became a career in 2008. Poetry has always been a hobby I indulged in during my high school days and as an adult in the privacy of my own home. I can write a poem at the drop of a hat—give me a subject. Love is my favourite topic, and loving and falling in love is my greatest inspiration.

It has become a fun hobby for me; making songs is a relaxing activity. Almost on par with a day at the cricket!

My music taste is broad. I enjoy a wide range of music, including rap, pop, hip-hop, blues, metal, rock, nu-metal, opera, jazz, and classical. Making Music since 2021 has been a fun hobby and a productive pastime, which I hope to grow into and produce more as life unfolds.

By 2023 after disruptions to my plans to study fashion I found myself studying my Bachelor of Arts (Music Production), with two compilations which had been heard across the world in the background on media platforms, a Shure microphone (SM58), Sony headphones (MDR-7506) and Shure X2U adapter I was producing compilations with the latest version Digital audio workstation (DAWs) from Ableton (highly respected professional music production software) and furthermore, moving into podcast production with new Shure technology.

Completing my Diploma in Music Production in December 2023, finalising the studies at the Diploma degree, as I have no real need to pursue the bachelor's degree based on the spectrum of my studies and the practical applications I would engage in. I transferred into the Fashion and Sustainability Diploma, which I initially enquired about and applied for. A Bachelor of Arts is an asset to my teaching background, should I choose to pursue it (which I do not), and I already have opportunities in the entertainment industry. I am an actress who can expand into music entertainment with the diploma, and the knowledge furthers Barbwire Noose's ability to connect with the Music Industry. The studies have upskilled and taught me the basics of the industry, enabling me to produce music or create my own tunes. My plans for using this Music Production Diploma are to create runway music for my brand, Barbwire Noose®. In 2024, I produced the debut television commercial for Barbwire Noose using skills acquired through these studies, and to date, I am thrilled to be able to pursue and create another one of my passions.

The studies were a bit of a pain in the arse, due to police forces' desperation to tarnish everything I touched with perjury. Having a few hard-drug-using teachers is also not so great. Especially, studying and travelling. These lazy, underqualified teachers, more focused on their own music pastimes and weekend partying in the lower levels of the music scene, are more concerned with their own interests than anything else. A few of my teachers were actually cool and accomplished, which provided great insight into what to expect as I entered the industry. The others literally just caused lawsuits stemming from defamation, turned perjury, and emotional distress with VICPOL. It is a sad, sick world when idiots get jealous over shit you haven't even accomplished yet. Alas, I am pretty confident in my abilities and have learned a great deal from the Diploma as a relatively new music producer.

I have an endless supply of poetry, some of which I am eager to set to music. I have always loved a good interlude on an album, so a few of my shorter favourite poems, I am sure, will be scattered through the music I put out to the world. I can dance most people off the dance floor; I used to be able to anyway, like bike riding, so I am really excited to see where my Music Production Diploma can take me. It's a new world, and I've started to make my pastimes into careers. They do say doing what you love is the best career path. At this point in my life, I have started to think that I should focus on fewer extracurricular activities and consider stopping my studies at some point. Both of which will never happen.

The study makes Music aspirations a reality and more serious than just a distraction for my mind. Bitter-sweet. Barbwire Noose® is involved with the heavy metal scene via the BRUTAL feature and sponsorships. Having shown a natural talent in the acting roles I've been cast in, I've seen the study as an across-the-board upskilling.

Making and studying music is taking me to a whole new level emotionally, and it's a good place, I feel. Only the gods know what the future holds for this space. Barbwire Noose is my baby, my One Love. Fashion is my passion. Perhaps we'll see my One Love branch expand into a record label under the trademark from another hobby. Another muse transformed into Enterprise, ultimately achieving progress towards a Better World.

Music will be my Muse until the day I die. My playlists, though long, will always flog certain songs for quite a while, and I'll always set the playlist to play sweet nothings to my partner as they get in the car. I've done this since my first boyfriend. Dread the day you're left with a breakup song after I get out of the vehicle. You know you're dumped.

Music uplifts, deflates, and over the years, I have witnessed music being manipulated as a form of psychological warfare. Bet those boys regret that now, considering I played songs back at STARForce, the CIA, and other military geeks on privacy invasion highs. These abusive losers would have fucked themselves in the head hearing the same music all the time, at least. Especially when I'd play complementary songs like 'She's a Genius' by JET and 'Machinehead' by BUSH. Manipulate those songs bitches! Compliments must have been driving the opposition crazy all the way.

Psychological warfare is so illegal and not a cool practice, yet the use of music as a weapon has been going on for decades—irresponsible shit. Do something better with your time; don't harass people because you think it's delving into their psyche. Technology is applied in the most manipulative of ways.

Music should be touching, relatable, uplifting, moving, emotive, and tell a story—sad, happy, or whatever you want it to be—but it should not be used to hurt people through warfare. Play a breakup song to your ex, don't hack the Bluetooth to try and get confessions because you have twisted ideas about people's lives. That's fucked up.

Music is not only a muse, a motivator, and a distraction, but also a long-term hobby that allows for a break from the seriousness of some days. I finish with 'Music Saves Lives', Corey Taylor (Slipknot, Stone Sour vocalist).

Chapter Seven
'Poetry'

GLASS HOUSES (06/06/2023)

What you see with your eyes,

These are pages of my life.

Not words in a book,

Not ink on paper.

You read pieces of my soul,

Pieces of Me.

The truth between the lies,

A thousand long-lost cries.

Curiosity,

Vulnerability,

An ability to dream.

To cry,

To live,

To sigh,

Barbwire Noose

To say all the things you wish you could say.

Those opportunities that melt away.

The you in me and the me in you.

Us two.

Apart in agreement,

Torn in disagreement,

With every word unsaid.

As I let you look in through the glass,

Know that I am looking back.

Like a recap,

Like judgment day.

The energy we exchange in this emotive state,

Will never go away.

The hate,

The love,

The intrigue,

The dismay,

Every time you look at that page.

You stare at me,

Anything But Ordinary

And I stare at you.

Judging on another,

With no real clue about each other.

In our shadowless glass houses,

We are both judgmental cowards.

No stones get thrown,

From either throne.

Yet within my scripture,

Shadow is clearly in the picture.

Created by your face,

On the page that it graces.

"You're making my words ugly with your shadow, which has no permanent reflection on what I have to say – Human Rights Matter."

Marcia Anita Hobbs (BNoose), 1984.

Lodge 406, Adelaide, AUS, Le Droit Humain.

Barbwire Noose

The Hollow Moon sings to the Sun

What is she they ask?

For she is Magic.

The speck of dust dazzling the sky to which we do not see,

The whispers in the night to which we only breathe,

The light shone upon the desert moon to which we never knew
came to be.

That something,

Nothing.

That dream in a nightmare,

The death of all our care.

She is an abyss,

Engulfed in an eclipse.

An illusion of a gift.

For she is you,

If you chose to shine,

As high as the sun is bright.

The endless night,

The epitome of might.

Anything But Ordinary

Everything that is mine.

That's what she is.

Marcia Anita Hobbs, 1984

Lodge 406, 11 February 2021

THE AIRPORT

They will meet you wherever I am not,

Whenever we don't get along.

However opportunity presents,

Forever.

For true love cannot be broken.

And they know,

They know by the look in your eyes,

The fade in your smile,

The doubt in your mind,

The jealousy on your face.

They will meet you wherever I am not,

And if you let them,

I am gone.

Barbwire Noose

(Written 20 March 2024)

8281 MILES

They sparkle,

Like a thousand tiny moons in the night sky,

They shine.

Out of reach yet every night there.

In solitude or sweetness,

Mourning or peace.

They sparkle in the night sky.

A thousand tiny moons,

Shining for me and you.

(Written 20 March 2024)

FEELING ALIVE

To fall in love is the ultimate sacrilege,

Born of this source,

Anything But Ordinary

We radiate light so bright,

So strong,

So timeless.

On a course of freedom and destruction,

We love life,

Love each other,

Love bounties and boundaries.

Power and peace,

A feeling so conflicting,

So true,

So me,

So you,

So us.

So nothing,

So everything.

That is love,

What's lost,

What's yet to come.

What stays,

Barbwire Noose

What goes,

Love flows,

Forever.

No matter what,

No matter who.

There is a me in every you,

And a you in every me,

My dear,

I love you.

(Written 21 March 2024)

ERIC x

In the quiet corners of the world,

Where the night is still,

And there is no breeze.

I feel you here.

In the calm of morning,

Under the sunrise of fire,

Anything But Ordinary

I see you here.

By the moon in the night sky,

Dazzling as the stars,

In a world full of faces,

Beautiful places and lust.

I choose us.

(Written 22 March 2024)

A BOY & A FULL MOON NIGHT

And I felt it flutter,

I felt a pulse,

You make me stutter,

And feel like I am lost.

The full moon bright,

You're my moon tonight.

You make it flutter,

My frozen heart shudders.

It makes me realise,

Barbwire Noose

I am alive.

Alive with you tonight.

(Written 23 April 2024)

HOPE

In times of discrimination,

We need a United Nations.

A world where one is all and all is one,

Not just a notion but a place for everyone in the Sun.

Below the moon,

Where man flies high.

With the birds and universe in the sky,

No child should starve nor cry.

Power.

Greed – when humanity is man's need.

Peace has no cost,

We are lost –

To be found,

Anything But Ordinary

Put our feet back on the ground.

Empowerment.

Unity.

Diversity.

Love.

Things created each day above.

For man to implement in times of need,

If only humanity could overcome man's lust for greed.

All in this room can make a change.

Maintain kindness and grace,

For the entire human race.

We are the people.

We Unite the Nations.

And it is as simple,

As no judgment or discrimination.

A kind word.

A smile.

All us can deliver,

To make Peace and Hope world-changingly bigger.

Barbwire Noose

Written as Beauty Queen Pageant title holder, Miss Australia United Nations 2018 for the Finals held in Jamaica. 27/07/2018

The following are untitled poetic notions, for me, for you, for someone. Enjoy x

I could live with just the money now honey,

So, what do I do, now that I've met you.

This veil of sweet lullabies, white lies, and unheard cries would ravage the heart so dark yet never disturbed the light.

Delicate – a statement from the outside,

Lost eyes and a slow demise.

Nothing whispers louder than lost innocence.

I promise you nothing in return for your promise of nothing but loyalty; your loyalty is fake and does not shake me.

As I am free, and though this freedom feels like a cage, it is you who has lost your way while I stand at your gate of hate.

Chapter Eight
'Protest'

Definition: a statement or action expressing disapproval of or objection to something. "The team lodged an official protest".

I have always signed petitions in protest of things I believed in or stood against. I have volunteered with protesting and petitioning charities, such as Save the Reef, against Factory Farming, and to stop caged egg sales, to name a few. Petitions are a great way to raise community awareness and prompt action, which in turn encourages government, local councils, or organisations to take action.

Daily (at times), I sign petitions in protest for change. Rallies are held at the Parliament House. Whistle-blowers globally write books. People's freedom to express democratic rights is on display in protest.

A petition is basically a request for action. The right to petition the Federal Parliament has been a fundamental right of citizens since federation, and it is the only way an individual can directly present grievances to Parliament.

Senate Petitions - The presentation of a petition to the Senate is a parliamentary proceeding and is protected by parliamentary privilege. The publication of a petition before presentation is not similarly protected.

House of Representatives petition - A petition to the House of Representatives (the House) is a formal request for action on a matter that falls within the House's jurisdiction.

The House Standing Committee on Petitions receives and processes petitions on behalf of the House of Representatives. Petitions to the House must comply with the rules and may be presented by a Member of Parliament or the Committee Chair.

Petition rules in Australia stipulate that your petition must provide a reason for making the request. The reason offers information to help people understand what you are asking for and why. Your petition reason must not include URLs or attachments; e.g., the language you use must be non-threatening (moderate in content) and limited to an easy-to-understand 250 words. E-petitions are restricted and can collect signatures online for 4 weeks from the date the committee approves the e-petition. This timeframe cannot be changed. The residence must be in Australia; your petition must be addressed appropriately if you are requesting something that the House of Representatives (the House) can do, typically something that falls under the responsibility of the Federal Government and not a state or territory government or a local council.

✓ A petition can ask the House to put a new tax on sugary drinks. (The Federal Government is responsible for taxes on food and beverages.)

✗ A petition cannot ask the House to change the laws for cats and dogs. (State and territory governments are responsible for domestic animal laws.)

✗ A petition cannot ask the House to change the days for rubbish collection in your suburb. (Local councils are responsible for rubbish collection.)

Protesting authority came naturally to me. I was brought up by strong-willed, rebel parents who practised the norms of living but didn't always live by them. My family never believed that the prohibition of marijuana was right and exercised their beliefs that marijuana is an herb, a plant to which we are all entitled to benefit from, and that we are all free to grow.

I grew up in a household where television (TV) viewing was strictly monitored, and as a child, I was taught not to believe everything I saw or heard on TV. My Dad was generally the household authority and the first person I rebelled against, outside of usually defying tyrannical, dictatorial authority.

The second instance of a rebel protest against authority was when I threw a softball at the teacher; she made me write an apology letter. She was mean and was allowing this boy, who had a crush on me, to be annoying to me – he constantly hit me in the arm for attention, and she did nothing but dribble shit justifications that I needed to understand his emotions, talking at me with her coffee camel breath. I thought to myself, You want me to understand his abuse and ignore my own feelings. What an idiotic leadership that is. I was in year seven at school and remember thinking, I'm out of here soon —so no more taking your shit, mean teacher. After three years of her strict manner, lack of consideration for my welfare regarding Mr Butler's crush, and her overall demonic persona, enough was enough for me, apparently, launching the ball with greater than usual enthusiasm. Mrs Paltridge was the second authority figure I significantly rebelled against. Vowing to all my schoolmates that I would move out of the dictatorship (at times) at home to freedom as soon as I obtained my licence, which I did, gaining my P-plates licence at the end of the year 2000. I moved out of home before my seventeenth birthday in 2001, living with my boyfriend's family at the end of school (2000), before packing up all my stuff and leaving the farm to live in the city of Mount Gambier.

It was two years later when I started standing up for the human rights of non-cognitive, disabled persons, when I was only nineteen, protecting the Human Rights of my peers from a government that irrefutably did not give a shit about them. Believe it or not, Mrs Paltridge had a disabled daughter, and I ended up as her child's carer. The callous teacher provided her daughter with a lovely home, yet clearly did not want people to know that this disabled person was her daughter.

"One child, one teacher, one book, and one pen can change the world." — Malala Yousafzai.

Protest takes many forms; sometimes it is as simple as saying no or saying, 'Enough is enough.' Then there are Tree sitters who camp in trees, send their shit on newspaper down to fellow activists to stop deforestation. Long periods where food is provided by means of a rope pulley system, with your double-bagged shit hanging under your bed – away from the nose. Literally excreting on paper - on your bed. What dedication and personal sacrifice. I learnt so much hearing about these genuine movements to save sacred trees and forest sites – our Earth's lungs. No sacrifice, smaller nor greater than that which I have made for Disabled persons' justice – nearly dying to stop a cover-up is taking protest pretty far. Most people would have and did give up on these tortured, disabled souls – tortured souls like mine. No enormity in comparison to Julian Assange's sacrifice for truth, transparency, and free speech. Yet, each and every movement, big or small, in protest is significant. Saving the Trees is more than a hippie thing, with Central Intelligence Agency (CIA) documents released showing deforestation is a military plan.

My activism had been low-key, really, a country girl speaking out for the vulnerable's rights, signing petitions and donations to good causes (money and time) - me just being me. Until the police forces' dirty cover-up of sex crimes was announced to the world. In 2010, I was a public figure in South Australia and Victoria with a significant global social media presence, utilising the brand Barbwire Noose and creating content to promote my fashion label. An entrepreneur and fashion designer with Barbwire Noose® and strategically aligned with relevant industries. By this stage, I had spent five years (since 2005) fighting for the rights of people with disabilities while living my private life and becoming an influencer through the brand Barbwire Noose®, and my activism had gained influence. Building a brand that stemmed from a Human Rights movement was against the status quo. Most activists were hippies, getting arrested, chained to trees, holding up signs, or standing naked, getting attention. The conventional approach was often not for me. For ten years, I fought alone for the rights of people with disabilities, with the brand Barbwire Noose unrecognised for its activism. I am actually kind of shy, confident, but anti-social, so becoming recognised in the struggles and efforts I was making for non-cognitive voices, my peers, and our peers, was overwhelming. The lack of media coverage of the cover-up was underwhelming, and in my disgruntlement, I expressed my detest via email.

Like the heavy metal scene, I was surrounded by people who had done something remarkable, often attended a protest, and even been locked up for it. My name became broadly known after the VICPOL torts of 2022. I was friends with whistle-blowers at this stage of life, had grown up around hippies, and interacted with all walks of life during my thirties while I intensely whistle-blowed governance sex crimes. I admired the anti-vaccination protest of these times, yet couldn't help but notice the judgmental hate generated in misunderstandings of the coronavirus (COVID). Personally, I see hate and division as the government's greatest weapon – you don't have to like someone for them to be right, yet people think you must want someone to support the truth. Logical fallacies are everywhere, like bigotry. Like other well-protested causes, it was dragged down by misunderstanding and judgment. The point of protesting the vaccination was about personal sovereignty. It wasn't about the vaccine or even science; it was individual health and freedom of choice. We should all have the right to choose whether to be vaccinated or not. The dictatorship to which forced vaccination is wrong, yet in this moment, people turned against their families with different opinions and picked at both sides of the science. Fighting for the exact causes —humanity, the environment, and our freedoms —yet people were not always supportive and looked for excuses to discredit one another. Ugly human nature is to dismiss what we do not understand, and this is non-evolutionary, too. I, myself, subject to these discriminatory practices in character assassinations, my interpretation of the ongoing surrounding lockdowns was very psychologically oriented. Looking from the outside in. What anyone can see, being objective, is the 101 of how governments trample over the people, deception, and division—creating spaces of doubt, judgment, segregation, and agitation. Spaces we allow because of jealousy, lack of understanding, entitlement, or greed, generally. Having extensively studied leadership, I know these factors often ruin teams: the want for recognition, others seemingly less worthy, unity for a day, and not in the good faith of maintaining humanity, no matter of colour, creed, or complexity—actions which could only have been driven by envy and solidified by a deep-seated, bitter jealousy. Blessed with endless opportunities, I found people (both male and female) would often judge me in both the metal and humanitarian scene, as I didn't dress the same as them all the time. I wore designer shoes, dripped in jewellery, called going to the toilet the bathroom and not the shitter – stuff like that. Judgmental people really piss me off, and my reaction is actually to protest their narrative of a box description. Whether that means you must wear black to be metal, look goth to enjoy Opeth (European heavy metal), wear tie-dye to be a hippie, or a poncho to be a protester, etc. Like the heavy metal scene, I can be both Metal and Barbie, which is exactly me. In my participation in pageantry competitions, I was described as "Rock Princess", which is a rather fitting description of my persona. Simple truths - Do you.

Too rich to be a protester, too prissy to be a goth. It seems I was too individual for these individualist and self-proclaimed non-judgmental groups; go figure. Luckily, it doesn't matter to my old soul.

Judgmental ideals aside, protesting on two fronts is tragic. Imagine protesting a cause and achieving more than the hippy with a vegetable oil-run vehicle, yet you must protest this dick for your right to protest. Adversity from cheap allies makes you want to leave them in their struggling misery of taking ten years to achieve what I could in two. Luckily, I'm not the bitter type, and I believe protest is about making A Better World, not about a name, a phase, or about making a martyr out of oneself.

"Never doubt that a small group of thoughtful committed individuals can change the world. In fact, it's the only thing that ever has."

Being held hostage to reckless endangerment, tortured by police forces covering up sex crimes, I was privileged to meet many like-minded people. Both influential and influenced by humanitarian movements.

Arrests and incarceration for activism are, unfortunately, routine when activists exercise their rights to free speech and protest.

I heard about musician Isabella (Izzy) Brown, founder of the nonprofit collective United Struggle Project, when I was at Tamara Date Farm in NT. One among many Amazing people that I was exposed to through the story of their journey to resolution - fighting for human rights and constitutional writ violations. Fighting for myself and my disabled peers.

A woman described as dedicating much of her life to protest, Izzy has organised and attended movements regarding Anti-uranium, Anti-weapon, logging, BHP, to name a few. She has squatted for shelter and negotiated homes for people experiencing homelessness in abandoned areas of Melbourne, Victoria.

Izzy is genuinely passionate about giving a voice to displaced people globally through music. Izzy is a rapper in the Melbourne hip-hop band Combat Wombat and co-founder of the Lab Rat Solar sound system, alongside Marc Peckham (Monkey Marc). It is always a privilege to get acquainted with passionate activists, as with whistle-blowers like David McBride; I felt compelled to write about these Individuals. This book's chapter is dedicated to protest and some ceiling smashers, movers, and shakers – People like me.

Izzy's son modelled for Barbwire Noose® threads with friends who had travelled to remote Australia to attend the Wide Open Spaces (WOS) Festival. The event was hosted in conjunction with the Tamara Date Farm Co-operative member, Monkey Marc. Izzy and Monkey Marc are an inspiration to local activists, touring Australia in a van powered by vegetable oil. Years later, a logging activist and cooperative member of the farm converted a truck to vegetable oil operations and travelled over 7,500 kilometres across Australia. A truck I travelled in, that can still operate on vegetable oil approximately ten years later.

Surrounded by some genuine environmentalists and passionate change-makers on the Tamara Date farm (as well as those mentioned earlier). Izzy, dedicated to humanitarian work, has a vast and humble story to tell. Self-proclaiming, with a suitcase-sized recording studio in hand, she travelled with her seven-year-old son, setting out on a tour to record and collaborate on tracks. Making music videos in the far corners of the planet in refugee camps, slums, prisons, and remote communities to bring these voices to the world.' What an incredible story. The United Struggle Project aims to produce media, including songs, music videos, and documentaries, recorded in the slums, refugee camps, and prisons of remote communities in Africa, the Middle East, Cambodia, and Australia. Izzy, described as a powerhouse by her friends and peers, is living life dedicated to fighting the Good fight. A soldier for society, ground level, and entertaining if you check out YouTube. So blessed to have crossed paths with such an Amazing Protester, Google the name Isabella Brown and get acquainted yourself!

Bauxau (Bau) Stone, a frail, elderly South African man of many outstanding achievements, claims to protest on behalf of Australian Indigenous rights. I met Bau at the Alice Springs YHA, where he would stay, taking a break from working the date farm. Bau introduced me to the Tamara date farm co-operative and suggested, during the stress of whistleblowing, that I should volunteer and indulge in the beautiful desert Oasis as R&R. Which I did – though I cannot say the stay relieved the stress. Indulging the slower-paced lifestyle and experiencing the characters and culture of the dusty outback was nice and a new experience – until it wasn't. My time at Tamara Date Farm, as discussed, occurred before I headed home to South Australia. Admittedly, I was slightly reluctant to accept an invitation to a location in the middle of nowhere, with minimal phone access and a majority of male residents. Accepting the invitation under reckless endangerment circumstances, unaware of the undermining agenda Bau and members of the farm had against non-cognitive and me, gaining justice against sex crimes. There was literally a group effort to take me down - reputational damage conspiring, by the sex offender sanctuary and its Labor government cronies.

Bau had openly admitted he'd been hiding for eight odd years on the farm after returning from Africa. He claimed his family was strongly Labor and friends with Kim Beasley. My admiration for the man who advocated for a group of Indigenous people to participate in a significant event in Adelaide, organised by the SA Government and Premier Don Dunstan, quickly dissipated when it became evident that his actions were politically motivated, rather than humanitarian. A performance by Indigenous persons that would never have occurred without Bau's sustained persistence to achieve equality of rights. A determination driven by the fact that he wanted to stick it up a Liberal Government minister as a Labor government devotee. In a Labor government, I was heavily involved in whistleblowing in 2023.

I interacted minimally with Bau on the farm. I realised quickly that something was not right about the entire situation when I was not initially provided adequate accommodation. All self-proclaimed, I found little articulated about Bau, even though he claimed in protest to have been dragged by police out of South Australia. A softly spoken man who enjoys alcoholic beverages, women, music, and good company. Making the best wood-fired pizzas on the farm. Unfortunately, all I witnessed was a broken-hearted man who hated his son and drowned himself with Alcohol. Alcohol, which drove him to call me a Nazi, police informant, belligerently, and to make numerous other defamatory claims. Claims, to which only a few months after Bryan Porker had sexually assaulted me and after spending weeks of R&R in an environment intentionally trying to provoke my CPTSD, I was apparently not supposed to defend myself against – my self-defence being arguing back with the belligerent old bullshit artist. Self-defence is a right, especially if you're being attacked. No matter whether that person is young or old, you are entitled to take reasonable steps to protect your personal safety under the law.

After visiting the farm, it was apparent why Bau was hiding out there. Protected by vested interests and a detest for the Liberal government shared by Labor government-employed and aligned cooperative members. Disappointing to learn that a place and people that sell an image as humanitarians, evidently, is a haven for bullies, sex offenders, and Human Rights violations.

The good people of Tamara Date Farm are great, yet overruled and overpowered by hate, greed, and dishonesty. You're only as good as the company you keep at times.

Anything But Ordinary

My protest, Which Involved Human Rights activism for resolution and seeking an apology for disabled persons who suffered from criminal negligence under the South Australian state Labour government of Mike Rann, Disability Minister Jay Weatherill, and politician Mark Butler, was promoted by Human Rights billboards across Adelaide by 2023. South Australia and the persistent pursuit of conventional resolution via communication and courts. Returning home from Tamara Date Farm after travelling and experiencing numerous persons engaging in affray activities to assist the police in a cover-up of paedophilia.

Irrefutable facts and results of freedom from tyranny are the ultimate goals of protest. Public disclosure is the ultimate accountability and protest against a cover-up. My autobiographies and the literature of whistleblowers globally are culture-changing and life-changing. The impact of the truth set free has paved the way for generations to come. As with all my autobiographies, a few unnecessary names are politely removed. Despite my opinion that we are all accountable for that which we do and do not do. All information is researched with support from verified documents, media articles, recorded events, and personal accounts, to the best of my recollection, knowledge, ability, and availability of facts. Persons expecting to read about themselves or others may be disappointed, as I do not write about fame grabbers fondly or at times at all in my Autobiographies. I have complete discretion regarding autobiographical publications under my name. If you were disrespectful and not genuinely invested in the truth, if you just wanted to discuss being a part of my life — whether positive, negative, or otherwise — you may be disappointed by your absence. Some people, as we discussed in the book, I decided I didn't actually like once they became more than an acquainted stranger (accused unconvicted sex offenders claiming reform, mean people, intoxicated/substance inhibitions, thieves, narcissistic personalities, immaturity, etc), so I took the first exit I could to get them out of life and away from foul efforts stealing fifteen minutes of fame, and either moved property or at least drove away. After all, these books are autobiographies and public disclosures; if you cannot tell the truth or have no conviction, I have no time for your nonsense.

I had dropped three bombshell autobiographies since witnessing a cover-up of sex crimes, which commenced in 2015 under AFP operations involving VICPOL and SAPOL. This book is my fourth.

In 2015, upon evidence of police covering up the sex offence committed by Kurt Slaven, I announced on record that I would write a book about the incident and the cover-up. Three years later, I started writing my first autobiography.

I intend to take Barbwire Noose® to the top – my sights are set on the United States of America, specifically New York. In turn, I have ambitions to make a positive impact in law enforcement there as well, if possible.

As God is my witness, the truest of words, the pen is indeed a weapon. This autobiographical series is a testament to the world's changing times and the importance of free speech.

Human Rights Matter – Always.

I believe governments are slowly eroding our right to protest freely. The right to peaceful assembly protects the right of individuals and groups to meet and to engage in peaceful protest. The right to freedom of association protects the right to form and join associations to pursue common goals. While it is not a direct offence to hold a protest on public land, a permit protects you from certain criminal charges, such as obstructing traffic or other pedestrians. All councils either strongly recommend or require local police to be notified if a large protest is taking place.

We must remember public land is OUR land. Crown land is OUR land. If the government didn't take OUR taxes, they could not fund law enforcement to wage war on OUR rights.

We, the People, will always outnumber those in power. It is your right to protest, and you should do so peacefully, because protest is a powerful tool that can create change. Protest speaks YOUR voice. Protest is Democracy, and the day that government bans protest is the day you live under a dictatorship, not under free world rule.

I have attended many protests. If I am in a position to join a cause I believe in, I will. No matter what I have planned. I will put my plans on hold and take time out to be a voice, to show support, and to be part of the change that makes A Better World. And you should, too.

April 27th, 2024, two days after my Birthday. The morning after I attended the ANZAC Day AFL match in Adelaide, South Australia, I was feeling the effects of late-night drinking. I stood at the foot of Adelaide Parliament House's door, next to a man who had stood against Domestic Violence (DV), a saviour to a neighbour let down by police, as I have been, not hating on police, though recognising the culture that dismissed the seriousness of abuse. Beaten for speaking out in her defence by the DV offender, he stood amongst us, by me, with his two dogs at this protest. To every man who attended this protest, I sincerely thank you, as the organisers and political speakers should have, but did not. This man, to me, is the most important in the crowd. I, myself, survived Domestic Violence and Sexual Abuse; this man was so profound. The 'NO More' protest marked statistics so high in Australia that it equated to severe violence – the loss of a life every four days. Tragic yet true, I felt every heartbreaking story: the Mourning, the pain, and productive anger in all its glory. The world will not change by words alone; be active, be brave, be loud and direct in your tone. Peaceful protest is a precious right, which speaks to the righteous and makes our lives better. Enough is Enough.

"Condoning the violence with your silence." – Marcia Anita Hobbs (BNoose).

Here's a relevant blog for this topic. Enjoy:

If you want to make noise in the world of Human Rights, you have to *shout*. You have to be relentless. You have to be raw. This isn't a game for the faint-hearted or the polite. It's a battlefield where silence is complicity and hesitation is defeat. I've been there, screaming into the void, wondering if anyone's listening. But here's the brutal truth: your voice *can* change the world. You have to know how to wield it like a weapon.

The Keys to Advocacy Success: What Nobody Tells You

Let's cut the fluff. Success in advocacy isn't about fancy speeches or perfectly curated social media posts. It's about *strategy*, *persistence*, and *authenticity*. You want to be heard? You need to understand the battlefield.

- **Know your audience**: Who are you talking to? Policymakers? The public? The media? Tailor your message to hit them where it hurts or inspires.

- **Master your message**: Clarity beats complexity every time. If your message is muddled, it's dead on arrival.

- **Build alliances**: No one changes the world alone. Find your tribe, your allies, your co-conspirators.

- **Use every platform**: From protests to podcasts, from fashion statements to published works, every channel is a megaphone.

- **Be unrelenting**: Change doesn't come overnight. It's a grind. A marathon. A war of attrition.

I've seen advocates burn out because they tried to do it all at once or because they didn't have a clear plan. Don't be that person. Be the one who outlasts, outsmarts, and outshouts.

What is Human Rights advocacy?

Let's get this straight. Human rights advocacy is not just about waving signs or posting hashtags; it's about taking action. It's a *deliberate* and strategic effort to protect and promote the fundamental rights that every person is entitled to. It's about fighting injustice wherever it hides - in laws, in policies, in social attitudes.

Human rights advocacy means:

- **Speaking up for the voiceless**: Those who are marginalised, oppressed, or ignored.

- **Holding power accountable**: Governments, corporations, institutions.

- **Educating and mobilising communities**: Awareness is the first step to action.

- **Pushing for systemic change**: Not just band-aids, but real, lasting reform.

This is why I partner with human rights advocacy organisations every day. It's not a hobby. It's a commitment. It's a fight for dignity, equality, and justice.

Using Fashion as a Form of Protest and Empowerment

You might think fashion and activism don't mix. Think again. Fashion is a language. It's a statement. It's a way to *wear* your beliefs on your sleeve - literally. When I launched Barbwire

Noose®, I wasn't just creating clothes. I was creating armour for the fight.

Here's how fashion becomes a megaphone:

- **Symbolism**: Designs that tell stories of resistance, pain, and hope.

- **Visibility**: Wearing your message in public spaces forces conversations.

- **Community**: Fashion connects people who share values and visions.

- **Economic power**: Supporting ethical brands funds the movement.

Imagine walking down the street wearing a jacket that screams defiance against injustice. People notice. They ask questions. You start a dialogue. That's power. That's advocacy.

Practical Steps to Amplify Your Voice Right Now.

The Power of Persistence and Personal Branding in Advocacy

Here's the raw truth: the world doesn't owe you attention. You have to *earn* it. And that means showing up every damn day, even when it's exhausting, even when it feels like no one cares.

Your personal brand is your megaphone. It's how people recognise you, trust you, and rally behind you. Marcia BNoose isn't just a name. It's a symbol of defiance, resilience, and relentless pursuit of justice. Your brand should be the same.

- **Be consistent**: Your message, your values, your presence.

- **Be authentic**: People smell fake a mile away.

- **Be bold**: Don't shy away from controversy or hard truths.

- **Be visible**: Use every platform, every opportunity.

- **Be a leader**: Inspire others to join the fight.

This is how you build a movement. This is how you amplify your voice beyond your own reach.

Your Voice is a Weapon - Use It

I'm not here to comfort you. I'm here to challenge you. Your voice is a weapon. It can tear down walls or build bridges. It can silence oppression or amplify the unheard. But it won't do anything if you keep it locked inside.

So, what are you waiting for? The world needs your fire. Your rage. Your hope. Your voice.

Get out there. Speak up. Fight hard. And never, ever stop. Because if not you, then who? If not now, then when?

Stop waiting for permission. Stop doubting your impact. Here's what you can do *today* to turn your voice into a force:

1. **Educate yourself deeply**: Know the issues inside out. Read reports, listen to survivors, and familiarise yourself with the relevant laws.

2. **Find your unique angle**: What's your story? Your passion? Your skill? Use it to connect with others.

3. **Create content that hits hard**: Write, film, design, speak. Be raw. Be real. Be unfiltered.

4. **Engage with decision-makers**: Write letters, attend meetings, demand accountability.

5. **Build a network**: Join groups, attend events, collaborate.

6. **Use social media strategically**: Don't just post. Mobilise. Organise. Challenge.

7. **Take care of yourself**: Burnout kills movements. Rest, recharge, and come back stronger.

This isn't theoretical. I've done it. I've seen the difference it makes when you stop waiting and start acting.

What the internet writes about me:

A life like a little rock princess at times, Marcia is a leader in legislative change, politics, and the business world. Protesting for change throughout South Australia and beyond, Marcia has dedicated her life to empowering those who feel they have no power or who genuinely lack it. A student of Policy and governance, Marcia contributes to sustainable changes within government and the fashion sector. Heavily invested in environmentally friendly fashion. Marcia is bold, outspoken, and an active change-maker. Her mission is 'A Better World'.

Marcia Anita Hobbs is a **Human Rights Activist, Fashion Designer, Author, and one of Australia's most controversial pillars of strength against corruption**.

What the internet says about these books:

What if the judgments we carry are more about others' projections than our true selves? How often do you let perception cloud your uniqueness?

"Anything but Ordinary Book Series - Judgement and Perception Have No Value Here" introduces Marcia Anita Hobbs's autobiographical series that challenges how society views judgment and perception. She shares raw stories, reflections, and experiences that dismantle conventional standards and celebrate authenticity.

Barbwire Noose

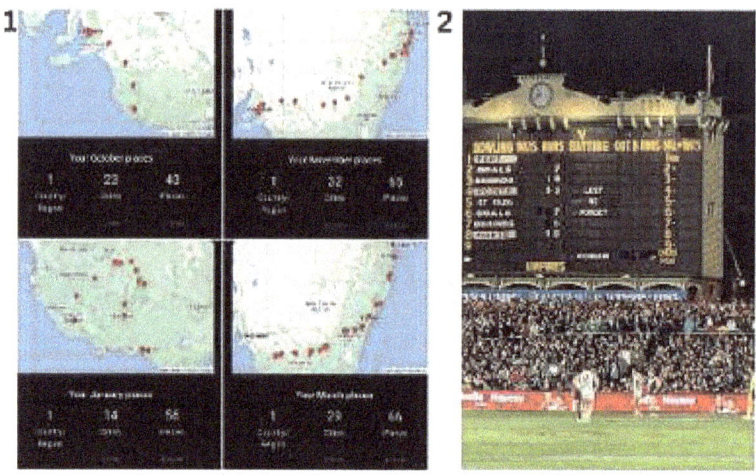

1. Regional Book Tour - Barbwire Noose Autobiography.   2. ANZAC Day Pt Adelaide VS St Kilda match.   3. Community event - MP Zoe Bettison.   4. Human Rights Matter billboards 5. 'NO More' Protest

Chapter Nine
'Truth VS Lies'

Be careful what lies you tell about me; some dick heads may be corrected in these books. Defamation is costly. Perjury is a criminal offence.

"The truth is incontrovertible. Malice may attack it, ignorance may deride it, but in the end, there it is." Winston Churchill.

If you have met me in the last ten years, you do not know me. You see a girl surviving an extraordinary emergency who never said the word 'cunt', such a vulgar word, until these years. If I spoke to you like that, I was distraught, or it was necessary, as that's the level of communication you engage with, understand, or deserve (in general). Judgement and perception have NO value here. Your opinion, based on lies, intentional meetings, and bullshit alliances, is all that you know. That's on you, not me, so my suggestion is you shut your mouth instead of feigning friendship for fifteen minutes of fame. I have but a few friends I can count on one hand. Those friends know I am a swim teacher, speak kindly and softly, and dress to impress whenever I can. Fashion is my life; you are the strife. Don't fuck with me for the Tiger and the Lion, maybe more powerful, but the wolf does not perform in the circus. I am the wolf; you are no more potent than Little Red Riding Hood.

I think the dumbest lie told about me came maliciously about in 2023, spread by a person to which I witnessed in an awkward Domestic Violence dispute—locking his partner outside of the house and gate in Alice Springs in the Northern Territory. This dick head spreading perjury that he was receiving death threats related to me and his house burning down. Blaming me for some random text messages sent while I travelled in remote Australia. A trip that saw me travelling over many remote roads and making stops at many remote towns with little to no phone service for over fifty per cent of the travel. The text messages from a phone number with no relation to me, I still don't know what phone number NTPOL claimed was mine. A police force so venal that they were extorted by local and international sex industries, as well as the countless crimes the Alice Springs NT police station has as its claims to fame. I co-piloted a BMW through narrow roads. The dimwit I travelled with took out two kangaroos, both headlights, and numerous birdlife. I've been travelling for a year in my little Kia Rio, without hitting a single animal, and with no damage to my car. The co-pilot was a predatory idiot, the idiot part I was aware of after a month of travel. His predatory tendencies were displayed after NTPOL, assisted by the AFP, engaged in perjury - detailed in UGLY HEROS: The Price of Unlawful Enforcement. A fun trip until it wasn't that started in Tasmania, where I saw Ben Harper, Angus and Julia Stone, and The Rubens perform at the Summer Salt Festival (20023), along with many other highlights. I had very few thoughts about the situation in Alice Springs, where I was to vacate the premises I resided. My lease was cancelled due to perjury, with everyone involved in the incident facing criminal charges related to this activity, including conspiracy and/or affray. My focus was on my brand, Barbwire Noose, and a potential sponsorship deal, as well as searching for a rental in South Australia until my tort's lawsuits were finalised. I was not focused on petty crimes nor blackmailed cops. The accusations coming at this time were ridiculous, outrageous, and honestly, so stupid that I could not help but add the humour that I am a terrible fire starter. This threat is not really my style (nor anyone I know, for that matter). Luke Fulton and Daniel Jacob Lowe (Born in NSW, Australia) were both guilty of Domestic Violence, which had been reported to NTPOL before their perjury. Both felons were well aware of the cover-ups the police were engaging in, as I authored public disclosures. These poor bullies, DV offenders against women, clearly just wanted fifteen minutes of fame, clearly knowing my situation, yet choosing to engage in perjury with the police anyway. To them I say – "Here you go, bucko, fifteen minutes of fame, just for you two losers right here!" Furthermore, in my UGLY HEROS Autobiography, violence against women is disgusting, and you boys are definitely that.

Irrefutably, the actions of the Mount Gambier police station in October 2020 under the Leadership of Phil Hoff (2019 – 2021), succeeded by Superintendent Campbell Hill (2021 – 2023), led directly to solicitation, and furthermore, an attempt at international sex trafficking. Perjury, among other crimes, by police forces, encouraging affray activities, and causing further grievous bodily harm. I have not and did not engage in solicitation; I would never be a prostitute. You'll see me in the papers as a serial killer before you'll ever read that I was a prostitute – that's how far from the truth this perjury is. The criminality that has occurred for years, even decades, stems from the Mount Gambier police station. Evident since 2015 during the Gordon Hamm homicide investigation; and when illegal acquisition took place in 2016, clearly ongoing due to malicious accusations with no basis or facts (perjury) which has circulated heavily since at least 2012 when paedophile pet of the police forces Luke Hubert Scheidl was circulating revenge porn in association with bikers, Paul Griffiths of SAPOL and the intentional cover up of police using prostitutes including children.

The Youth Hostel Australia (YHA) during the six (6) month period from the end of 2022 - 2023 in Alice Springs, where I witnessed, was unsafe for young women—harassment, food theft, and even sexual harassment rife within long-term residents and short-term travellers. I had not stayed long in a hotel accommodation or a backpacker's hostel before. This experience put me off backpackers altogether and caused much emotional distress after NTPOL perjury set in throughout the complex.

I addressed numerous issues with Management as soon as it became apparent to me and another volunteer member that the managers were not good people. The perjury further concretised this, which they engaged in with the YHA corporation director and other corporate representatives, which immediately caused me emotional distress. Personally, I was bullied by Alex Schneider, partner of Anna-Lena von Hohenegg-Quittek, and their creepy bald henchmen after reporting the questionable standards and criminality. The contents of my concerns were outlined to upper management, for the most part, as follows:

Dear Tracey,

I am writing to you regarding the severe circumstances of my stay at Alice Springs YHA. To start with, the stay seemed fine. The hostel has a swimming pool, music plays during the day, and these international hostels are said to have a safe reputation. Not this one. I watched a few odd goings on before I was told about a French lady who was asking for someone to take her to Uluru. A friend of the German managers at the facility offered to drive the French traveller, much younger than her chauffeur (an old, seedy Indigenous man who was a permanent resident at the YHA Alice Springs Hostel). This individual is a man who has regularly; long-

term stayed at YHA Alice Springs for approximately a decade. He is sold to travellers, including myself, as a good man by the Managers. I am not surprised the French lady trusted 'Uncle' to drive her to the Iconic landmark. A mural of the Indigenous man holding the daughter of the managers is painted on the wall; she had no reason to believe this man was a predator. Unfortunately, he is. Uncle told the French traveller that once she was isolated in the car, he would tell the French victim that it would take three days to travel approximately four hundred kilometres. Under duress, the French lady was told she had to sleep on the side of the road with Uncle as they travelled. Upon returning to the YHA Alice Springs, the French backpacker reported the incident, claiming an attempt at sexual assault. Instead of encouraging the French lady to report Uncle to the police, the Managers alerted Uncle of the complainant and her desire to report Uncle. Asking their Indigenous sex offender-level friend to stay somewhere else for the time being. I witnessed him leave and regularly return during my time at this hostel. The managers allowed him to return periodically to do laundry, use other facilities, and scope out potential victims, as I witnessed.

The Managers of the facility alerted two sex offenders that they had been reported during my short (approximately a couple of months) stay. I witnessed a horde of permanent residents, which I thought was odd, and then, upon visiting the website, I noted permanent residency is against YHA policy.

These matters concerning, I then witnessed Alex approve of Alice Springs resident stalker, who at this time self-proclaimed himself as a mentally unstable nurse that has harassed vulnerable women to stay the night. Alex's friend Dave (who works at the service station across from Hungry Jack's) is friends with stalker Sean Davis. Dave and I had discussed my concerns about Sean Davis, as I had seen him stalking me weeks before he was invited to stay at the YHA. Recorded on YHA cameras and also reported to SAPOL police, before the managers aided and abetted the criminal conduct. Dave knew he (Sean Davis) had stalked me when I worked as a bar attendant at Alice Springs casino. I believe Dave had told Alex, and Alex knew this when he booked Sean Davis to stay. I am single (relationship status), travelling alone from Alice Springs to Adelaide, South Australia.

Managers Alex Schneider and Anna-Lena von Hohenegg-Quittek, for over half a decade, Dave claims, have allowed him to stay permanently. A non-paying resident, he claims, who volunteers his time babysitting, not working within the YHA facilities like other volunteers - including myself.

Dave is waiting for the caravan behind the manager's house to permanently accommodate him, outside of staying permanently in the YHA rooms.

When the stalker was booked in last week, by this stage, I had had numerous items stolen from my property, including food from the kitchen, items in my room, and my laundry basket. One of the thieves was another friend of the management. I don't know his name, but after stealing my food, he was allowed to stay on despite stealing the eggs in the kitchen in front of the camera. Another girl, Amy, who appears slightly slow (intellectually), was also having lots of her food stolen, she told me.

The activity and vibe of the place is odd, and evidently, women in particular are not safe under this management to stay. I witnessed old men purchasing alcohol for much younger women, which was obviously to take advantage of these drunk girls. One regular resident, Bryan Porker, who is proud of his silver fox reputation at this YHA, and a drug dealer to the Managers, sexually assaulted me, which I have reported to the police, and moved rooms due to this activity. The move almost instantly sparked harassment from the Managers who were aware I was staying until the end of May, yet they started to badger me about dates.

When Sean Davis, self-proclaimed stalker, was booked in to stay oddly into the YHA, just before I was due to go back home to SA. I knew the managers were harassing me personally and had intentionally chosen to aid and abet a stalker. A man who actually resides in Alice Springs, a man who never regularly appeared at the YHA, turning up at the hostel after I was booked in for a short stay before returning to South Australia. Numerous excuses and gaslighting occurred when I called out this decision. Cutting my stay short by two weeks after thefts, felons, and blatant drug dealing were rife.

To make matters worse, I was awake most of this night, not only tossing and turning but on high alert because the door to my room was being left open by a German volunteer, and seemingly from interactions, a friend of Anna, the manager. The volunteer whom my friend and I discussed was clearly encouraged to leave the door unlocked, as in over three months she had never done this before. Malicious and intentional actions to cause me extreme emotional distress.

I reported the stalker staying at the facility to the police and leaving this YHA on Friday.

The managers are also friends with ICE cook and drug dealer Pete Lowe, whom I reported to the police in 2021 after I became aware of his activities. I am writing to you with grave concerns about the state of Alice Springs YHA management.

If you would like to discuss the matters further, my contact details are....

After writing this letter, the operations manager contacted me, initially focusing on the alleged perjury committed by police and management, before addressing my concerns. I thought they would be addressed seriously. The truth is that management allowed me to be bullied in front of other YHA guests and encouraged perjury, which had damaging consequences. I issued a cease and desist order, demanding an apology within fourteen (14) days, after which I would seek legal action against defamation and YHA for causing emotional distress, as well as perjury and other associated criminal charges. With police working more against me than for the truth and integrity, obtaining criminal charges should have been easy, yet it clearly was not.

The YHA had not apologised nor paid any costs for their part in recklessly endangering my life, intentionally conspiring with others to peddle malicious perjury of sex work with no basis or facts, half a decade after condoning sexual harassment. Criminal negligence is a primary duty of care-related offence. The YHA advertises an environment on their website that claims to be Friendly, creating unique, sustainable spaces with just the right amount of modern comfort in safe, welcoming environments, giving you the freedom to explore. After a year of numerous perjury cases (at the time of this publication's print), I expected the AFP to charge persons involved in perjury and affray-related offences appropriately. Wanting a sincere written apology from YHA Australia as well as criminal negligence compensation at the least. YHA Australia ceasing operations in Australia is the most desirable outcome after they fail to address criminal conduct endangering my life.

I had spent many nights uncomfortable. Dealing with ongoing trauma, Complex PTSD, and a large scale of people moving around, which I never deal with in the privacy of my own home. Safe in my own place, protected from society's criminals until the police, lying under oath, and SAPOL's criminal negligence left me recklessly endangered, in an extraordinary emergency, and vulnerable circumstances.

Friday, May 12, 2023, was one of the most uncomfortable nights of my life, spent at the YHA. All due to police forces' perjury, freemasons, and Dave Kyriacou (SAPOL ID 40657) writing numerous false statements, which resulted in personal promotions within SAPOL out of the backs of child victims and seemingly blackmailing politicians and judges for social, legal, and political gains, as well as false incarceration. Bribery rife amongst venal married men; if they were not hiding infidelity, they were hiding homosexual tendencies, paedophilia, or STDs. These issues should not have been my problem for a decade. However, due to the cover-up between 2014 and 2016, and beyond, by SAPOL, VICPOL, and the AFP, these individuals, who were felons and foes, and the fundamentally flawed, maliciously intentional investigations and ongoing matters became my problem. A problem of criminal negligence by police forces, which was exacerbated by the YHA activity, followed by Airbnb, National Storage, etc, all irrefutably guilty of duty of care, criminal negligence – National Storage guilty of insurance fraud to aid and abet a cover-up of sex crimes. Many individuals receiving financial gains for crimes are actually receiving the proceeds of crime.

The truth was that in 2023, I was literally passing through Alice Springs, NT, like a tourist. Having returned to South Australia in September 2022, I collected my mail from home and travelled back to the state for some rest and recovery (R&R) after being falsely incarcerated. I had the short-term rental lease in place after flying out to New York, USA, at the end of 2022. Being met by torts in Hawaii, USA, incited by Australia, an invitation to travel to Tasmania with two randoms from Alice Springs, whose reputation amongst many was said to be safe enough, was appealing, as it would have been to most outgoing and adventurous types in my position. I had literally only had a three-month break, still writing, designing, and releasing products with Barbwire Noose®, just not working external employment, such as swimming teaching or at the casino, as I had been. I needed to recover from the extraordinary level of torts - police harassment, sexual abuses that had been engaged for a sex crimes cover-up. I had enrolled to study, which police forces disrupted to try and solidify perjury and push me to the refuge of suicide after such humiliating and dehumanising torts. I travelled down to Tasmania and up the east coast of Australia at the start of 2023. Spending New Year's Eve 2022 and New Year's Day 2023 at home in South Australia.

A bit more about the truth of being stuck in the NT due to the floods at the end of 2021, washing the roads away, I had to emergency reside in the city of Alice Springs, Northern Territory, for most of 2022. The visit to NT after travelling interstate for a couple of months at the start of 2023 allowed me to tie up loose ends (reports with the police, disability sector information, and saying goodbye to people) after months of jumping back into work with my brand. Despite my plans to only rest and relax, I am a sole trader and the manager of Barbwire Noose®, which had its Autobiography released despite my being falsely incarcerated - a clear disruptive measure by police. I had spent the end of 2022 working on my brand's book, with the e-Pub book releasing as a download at the National Library of Australia and globally (2022/2023). I profusely proofread the book to the best of my ability after being traumatised by extraordinary illegal torts involving the CIA, USA. The travel to Tasmania and along the East Coast was technically work-related. I spent thousands of dollars and a considerable amount of time touring and creating media for a Barbwire Noose sponsorship deal, and, like many others, I thought Bryan was an alright guy, as described a little in the ABO book 1. A good impression, which ceased when it came to my attention that Bryan Porker was not just involved with the legalisation of the drug marijuana in Australia, but he was also a sex pest who committed numerous crimes against my person. ABO book one was released as an e-Book manuscript, author proof, consisting of quite absent grammar and some spelling errors) in the National Library of Australia. At the same time, Bryan wanted fifteen minutes of 'Big Brother' (the TV Series) fame – that fifteen minutes of fame is now the 'Big Brother' of the AFP (police forces). Spending three months basically travelling after only three months of R&R, where I was committed to finalising The Story Behind the Brand BARBWIRE NOOSE® ready for print, was an enviable feat and half my luck until Bryan Porker sexually assaulted me. I was recovering from the trauma of false incarceration until this sponsorship prospect re-traumatised me. This escalated my emotional distress, which was further exacerbated when SAPOL failed to take an adequate statement, resulting in further criminal negligence and further sexual harassment. Dave Kyriacou (SAPOL ID 40657) is irrefutably guilty of criminal negligence, entrapment, and perjury resulting in sex crimes committed against my person.

Staying at the YHA Alice Springs, NT, was always a temporary solution to an extraordinary emergency created by felons Luke Fulton and Daniel Jacob Lowe (Born in NSW, Australia). The accommodation was a recommendation and a decision made not by choice, but due to these remarkable emergency circumstances. I wanted to attend a scheduled meeting about the Disability Royal Commission (public interest) in Alice Springs, to which The Story

Behind the Brand, BARBWIRE NOOSE®, was a submission. This is my reason for being in Alice Springs until May 2023.

The YHA is a long discussion about truth versus lies. Other relevant truthful details of the accommodation are that it was booked via a friend (Bryan Porker) of the managers, who had been friends with these German-descended managers for years. After witnessing a few unusual occurrences, I was informed about a French lady who was seeking someone to take her to Uluru. I knew this place and facility were not managed by good-quality people. Yet, I only had a short period until I travelled back to South Australia after the Disability Royal Commission discussion. Good people don't aid and abet stalkers, assist harassment, or engage in affray offending, drug addicts, in particular, ICE addicts do. The manager was close friends with an amphetamine/ICE dealer, Cook, who is accused of paedophilia against an Indigenous girl – Pistol Pete. The felon known to NTPOL, SAPOL, and VICPOL is named Pete Lowe. The truths about the ongoing nature of this YHA are shocking. Police aiding and abetting this activity, which has catastrophic legal ramifications for all involved, yet SAPOL, VICPOL, and NTPOL, overseen by the AFP, continued to commit these torts. Reece Kershaw, clearly, on some level, assisted VICPOL in not paying out the torts I was owed in 2023. Despite court records acknowledging false incarceration by VICPOL. I knew the Commissioner, Reece Kershaw, was aware of my case, as I had personally emailed the

AFP after being released from false imprisonment in September 2022.

To make matters worse, the YHA managers committed perjury with police claiming that the sex offender Bryan Porker and I were in a relationship, which the CIA/and or felons relayed to my ex-fiancée incarcerated in Berkeley County Detention Centre, and Travis Paul Enmon Jr (DOB16JAN1989) then also engaged in the perjury, making claims about myself and Bryan Porker in writing via SmartInmate/Jailmail communication. An old man with whom I had discussed the YHA managers, as well as myself, discussing Travis numerous times to clarify the status of my relationship with Bryan Porker, shows that this perjury was intentional and malicious. Travis had run the Gypsy Jokers, Bandidos, Comancheros, and Hells Angels agendas for years, so I was not surprised by his perjury. Yet I was surprised that he would be stupid enough to put it on record when I was communicating with the FBI and leaving Travis open to be charged with perjury and affray by the Feds. At the same time, he was incarcerated for domestic violence. What a fucking idiot. The YHA managers were under no misconception that I was never involved with their friend. Every liar named here knew they would be named and shamed in a public disclosure, yet all these dick heads committed felonies anyway. Go figure.

Another liar who had been a Gigolo in Germany, he confessed after a few weekends hanging out with me. His name is

Kiki McCoy. A bloke smart enough to back off when I told him, but dumb enough to try and ask for money out of me due to an OnlyFans post he approved (yet the CIA deleted) where you could barely see his head between my legs. A post made to piss off Travis, which Kiki knew all about, as I had to provide a photo of him with ID and a written approval for the post, which he allowed to be digitally created. The post clearly pissed off Travis, who was in jail, getting his criminal friends to spy on me – after engaging in perjury about old men, prostitution, and promiscuity. The dickheads in 2023 did not cease.

This 2024 truth brings a new breed of stupidity from VICPOL, known as Titus, who initially sought a relationship despite my stating I was engaged, which was a lie, but he didn't know that at the time. From the no to a relationship, this cut as muscle show rock climber exposed as a part-time Gigolo, like (Kiki), just wanted sex. Sex, which he claimed 'they' - law enforcement encouraged. After scoring the guy based on his ability to climb some of the most challenging climbs at the Arapiles in Victoria, Australia, and his having had half a dozen showers before I touched him, I was bored with him. The bloke just banged on me like I was a pincushion, which was not fun. I, after Titus, a UK national, ended up in the shortest relationship of my life with another nice yet lost man named Eric, who you can read briefly about in UGLY HEROES The Price of Unlawful Enforcement. Sounds slutty, I know; the international engagements were strategic as Travis was still claiming we were engaged, trying to fuck up my visa application – the perjury has caused heaps of stupid situations and complications.

Another relevant truth is I would never have gotten vaccinated if I were aware of the extent to which the police planned to tort me. I received the vaccination in 2022 to board the plane to New York, which was no longer required as of 2024. This fact is a compensable assault, evidently by both countries, as the CIA jabbed me with a tuberculosis vaccination in Hawaii, USA. Unless they admit to accessing my health records without authority, this is a medical health risk for anyone who has recently been vaccinated, which luckily, I had not.

Globally, in the context of COVID-19 (coronavirus), it can be said policing had a "sense of impunity and no accountability – not only no accountability to the community, but no accountability to other police." The Second World War proved this a century ago. The fact the American authorities assisted VICPOL in their tort shows a distinct case where accountability is irrefutable. Yet, a year later, both countries were trying to cover up their criminal torts of harassment and false incarceration. Police enforced the need for compulsory vaccination during the COVID-19 (coronavirus) period, as well as the lockdowns, and are the most complicit idiots for money and power I've been exposed to on this earth. No One should have been forced to receive the coronavirus vaccination, especially when pharmaceutical companies profited from the pandemic. A health crisis should never result in a profit, especially when the virus was produced by scientists, just like the vaccine. The World Health Organisation's sense of impunity and lack of governance accountability shows a dangerous standard for any New World Order or One World agenda plan.

In 2015, a police officer, called Paul Arthur Griffiths (SAPOL ID 38683), made false allegations against me that I was a prostitute. Yes, this is a fact, and I have been informed that this is why SAPOL never releases my FOI (Freedom of Information). Perjury on record with SAPOL, which amounted to these torts, was influenced by his Gypsy Jokers alliance with the sex industry and paedophile Kurt Slaven. Both men have a background in Navy service. This perjury was engaged after he shared vital evidence in the homicide case of Gordon Hamm, encouraged by STARForce, resulting in a further chain of causation due to SAPOL criminal negligence, and my life was left in an extraordinary emergency. I have never been involved in the sex industry on any level. A repeated truth - this lying under oath spread by police officers for over a decade resulted in grievous bodily harm (rape, sexual harassment, and assault), plus years of my constitutional rights violated and severe reckless endangerment.

The truth is, the police have been trying to play the Hells Angels in Australia, as with the CIA, for decades, whilst claiming to run the sex industry and many other biker gangs. Yet in 2020 - ongoing, police forces across Australia and the USA spread perjury that I was a Hells Angel, which they escalated with claims about a jumper they knew was not mine. WTF kind of lie is that?

The homeless lie. The truth is, I have always had a roof over my head; however, while travelling in Australia, I did camp. Yet, I have never been the definition of 'homeless', and despite my estranged relationship with my parents, I can always go home to Mt Gambier, South AUS. That stated, numerous government departments and police documents have claimed I am homeless, including Centrelink. This perjury has been building for years, despite tenancy disputes, lease agreements, and a literal agenda by the government to make a whistle-blower homeless, destitute, and induce the refuge of suicide. I might as well be Nikola Tesla. Over the years, I have spent fighting for Human Rights, constitutional rights, and justice against severe, life-threatening corruption (malfeasance) and institutional abuses in extraordinary emergencies. My FOI also shows perjury labelling me with 'no fixed address', which not only has criminal charges implications stemming from perjury but also has hefty financial repercussions, especially after the illegal acquisition of my home based on perjury involving government agencies, HomeStart. My property, sixty-nine Penola Road, Mt Gambier, South Australia, registered to Barbwire Noose Corporation and has been my sole trader business address for nearly two decades. The illegal acquisition is a breach of my Human Rights, especially Article 17: Everyone has the right to own property alone as well as in association with others.

No one shall be arbitrarily deprived of their property.

Plus, Articles: 3 Everyone has the right to life, liberty, and the security of a person. Article 5, No one shall be subjected to torture or to cruel, inhuman or degrading treatment or punishment. Article 6: Everyone has the right to recognition everywhere as a person before the law. Article 30: Nothing in this Declaration may be interpreted as implying for any State, group, or person any right to engage in any activity or to perform any act aimed at the destruction of any of the rights and freedoms set forth herein. As well as my constitutional rights to a fair trial if I am being accused of sex work, which is perjury by police in a cover-up of their own, and the governance of sex crimes.

To cover up for the paedophile offence committed against my person, the police not only required people to believe their perjury, but they also needed to recruit felons to help them spread the perjury. The homelessness aimed to make me look like a drug addict, as drug addiction is often associated with prostitutes. No one cares about a prostitute, which I have witnessed firsthand. The facts that community members think they are above drug addicts, prostitutes, etc, are irrefutable and abhorrent. This plot furthermore engaged to cover up Kurt Slaven's sex crime committed against me as a minor while he was on duty, was in hopes that I would not be seen as a victim, instead viewed in society as a felon, to which society often disregards justice for. The torts and perjury engaged after VICPOL falsely incarcerated me in support of SAPOL criminal negligence escalated under the AFP overseen homicide of Gordon Tearonui Hamm, which resulted in my home's illegal acquisition and STARForce covering up a plot where police used me as rape bait for decades. The detailed truth of SAPOL 'rape bait' felonies are contained in Autobiography UGLY HEROS.

The perjury that I like older men is a very emotionally distressing and disgusting lie. I like men around my age, preferring them to be one to three years within my age range. All of my boyfriends before the homicide of Gordon Tearonui Hamm and this cover-up plot had been around my age. SAPOL required this perception that I liked older men to try to justify Kurt Slaven's paedophilia, and Paul Arthur Griffiths (SAPOL ID 38683) perjury. For years, I have been psychologically tortured by police and sex offending gangsters alike, with the presence of old men encouraged by police to engage with me, which, before this extraordinary emergency, where police and government are engaging in a sex crimes cover up, I had no history of hanging around with as friends or dating. A dangerous level of affray activities, perjury, and criminal negligence, which caused bodily harm (rape), psychological trauma, false incarceration, and a complete breakdown of the family unit. Family members with whom I now rarely speak, and some I refuse to talk to for the foreseeable future.

Rumour has it I have cheated on all my boyfriends... the truth. I tried very hard to break up with each and every one of them before my actions took the turn to replace them. I couldn't exactly move out of my own house now, could I? That being said, this is not a rumour. It is true I technically have cheated on all my boyfriends, even though the 'cheating' notion was aided and abetted by the boyfriend who would not leave when he was asked.

Am I attracted to police officers? ABSOLUTELY NOT. The truth behind this damaging perjury and reckless rhetoric's escalation is entirely police driven. David Kyriacou (SAPOL ID 40647), who has a recorded history of sworn (as a police officer) false statements, two that I have seen, where he has committed perjury against myself under oath after trying to flirt with me in 2015, is evidently mentally unstable – not to an excuse level, the blokes stalking and obsessive tendencies couple by his obnoxious and disproportionate reactions show the bloke a the least needs a holiday. Cou Cou, like this man has acted crazy around me. Convinced of lies, these allegations are preposterous. The defamation turned perjury on court records and stated to fellow police officers started with SAPOL and was spread by persons who care not for the sexually assaulted disabled victims under the government's justice nor the truth. Law enforcement is riddled with seedy men and sex offenders. The truth is, I have never dated in good faith a police officer. I kind of actually hate cops. I definitely hate the occupation and have no respect for the job, basically. Technically, I have reported all police officers with a history of physical interaction with me for various forms of ethical misconduct and criminal conduct. The most recent case of a detective of Port Pirie, South Australia, who pulled my hands into his cock three times, before squashing me by mounting me on the couch in 2025 during a false arrest.

In 2021, my family, for the second time, tried to lure me into their physical presence by saying my Nanna was in the hospital and could die. I wasn't told which Nanna, and my Indian Nanna did die. I will never forgive them for this activity. Furthermore, my fucked in the head family were happy not to see me at the funeral or discuss her will with me. They are all revolting opportunistic scabs. My Nanna would not be rolling in her grave, as she knows the realities of her children. That said, I know she's proud of me for calling out their lies and greed. After years of gaslighting, victim-blaming, narcissism, and manipulative lies, I said no to visiting the hospital before whomever of my Nanna's died in 2021, thinking this plot was another game from my dad's mother, who had twice faked that she was on her deathbed. I vow to see none of my Nannas upon their deathbed after this, as I was robbed of attending Nanna Unger's passing away and funeral. The last of my Nanna's is my Hobbs family's Nanna, and after years of their psychological games and the plot surrounding my beloved Indian Nanna. She will die without my presence and attendance at her funeral. Rita Harding, my Hobbs Nanna, has always looked down on my Indian family and Indian Nanna, and I despise this attitude. I have requested to be removed from all wills and wish to have no further involvement with anyone who may be persuaded by malicious accusations with no basis or facts about me. My Indian Nanna expressed love even if I had been a prostitute, which is more than I can say for the majority of my family, who have shamed our name and my Nanna's good Christian values. Love you lots, Mavis Unger, R.I.P. Curry Queen. I Love You.

Fucked up facts, hey. I don't consider these people to be family or human most days. This blatant disregard for my Nanna's welfare and the years that they spent squabbling over percentages of the house they were entitled to are disgusting, despicable shadows of the people who raised me. The words of others who have witnessed your disgusting behaviour are also at a loss for words in describing the enormity of the low that you are.

Clearly, my parents took whatever Nanna willed to me, like they did when Dad's stepdad passed. I asked for nothing; I certainly gave you no permission to keep what was not given to you, though. Taking things from the dead that others wished for is a curse, not a blessing.

Robert Harding's will - I have never seen it and don't care to, yet my parents pocketed the $500.00 apparently willed in his name. My Uncle, GREEDY AND VENAL, Greg Hobbs, to this day commits tax fraud illegally claiming my Qantas shares when we were clearly estranged and he's never had permission to do so - FACTS.

I know nothing of Nanna's will (sick of hearing about it, just as I was when she was alive!) and made it clear that I wanted to claim nothing, while the vultures sold the paid-for house and looted her belongings. I hope that it was respectful. I doubt it if the death had to be a secret; it shows the squabbling got worse in her passing, not better. Bittersweet to have missed such a significant event. Glad I wasn't around for the aftermath of greed.

Meanwhile, my family was part of circulating malicious accusations with no basis or facts, intentionally at this time, clearly to take more than they were entitled to from a dead person.

Truths about my birth and about my birthday. I was conceived in a Volkswagen Combi by my Mum, Anita Mavis Unger, and my dad, Michael Stanley Hobbs. I was born in a taxi on the way to the hospital in Rose Park, Adelaide. There is no hospital there. My parents literally recorded the location on my birth certificate.

There's been a lot of controversy surrounding the year I finished school and when I obtained my licence. The fact is that I received my Learner's licence immediately upon my sixteenth birthday in 2000. Technically, the day before, as Anzac Day is a public holiday, the registration office processed the paperwork a day early for me. In October 2000, I obtained my P plates after six months. For over a decade, I proudly kept my driver's licence expiry as my birthday, a public holiday – Anzac Day. I drove to high school as soon as I obtained my P plates. Driving my friend, who was yet to get her licence, home from High School in Mount Gambier for the last few months of Year 12 in the year 2000.

Navy forces, the CIA, and organised crime, due to military links, are the only persons currently with the invisible technology (SAIC Technology). New York journalists published the technology. I witnessed this technology first-hand in my property, 69 Penola Road, Mount Gambier, South Australia, in 2014. This technology is utilised by paedophile associated criminals globally. The CIA knows organised crime has this technology, yet the CIA doesn't really seem to make the technology and criminality associated with the tech broadly known. The illegal application of this technology evades accountability by authorities. It has been engaged for years by criminal organisations and governments in psychological warfare attacks against citizens, including the Genocide of military personnel mainly. Genocide, among other things, is the killing of people by a government because of their indelible group membership (race, ethnicity, religion, language). The technology is used for espionage and certainly needs to be reined in regarding its applications and who it is administered to.

The truth about superannuation and you. Government departments have interfered with my superannuation for literally decades. As a government employee, I hold a SuperSA superannuation account. All my superannuation was rolled into this account. Additionally, I've held a REST superannuation account and a HOSTPlus superannuation account. With no basis or legal grounds, Australian police forces have communicated maliciously with ALL of my superannuation accounts, trying to obstruct my financial stability during the entire acknowledged cover-up. The best thing you can do with your superannuation is to invest it in yourself and use it when you want or need it, if possible. I know from experience that the government and superannuation companies would rather keep your hard-earned money upon your death as opposed to giving it to you.

Over the years 2020 to 2023, SAPOL police classified the sex crime of paedophilia by Kurt Slaven against me as Ethical misconduct. The Integrity Commission and ICAC are involved in the resolution; it is irrefutable that ICAC (established in 2012) has been protecting SAPOL sex offenders since its establishment. Pictured at the end of this chapter is the response in writing from the

Major Indictable police prosecution branch, SAPOL Mitch Daily, who happily tried to dehumanise me in the Major Indictable Unit, accepting and declaring the sex crime of paedophilia on duty as an ethical police matter.

Gaining publishing contracts to print while whistleblowing, most people thought, was an achievement and a blessing. The truth is, it was not half the time. Every book publisher I approached treated my books as an investigation, rather than evidence. The book was delayed, or, as with In-House Publishing Australia, the publication was withdrawn due to government pressure. Austin Macaulay Publishers, which has a questionable reputation when you Google them online, caused so much disruption to the print that I published the e-book myself. Austin Macaulay Publications has caused emails of psychological abuse and much emotional distress to the point where there is much email evidence that I was seeking other publishers and did not want them to profit from my publication after causing me much suffering, parting ways with this publisher in 2025 after investing in advertising, which included the publisher's branding.

The truth is, the Australian Army has a history of sexual violations in said battle and in-house. Most people say all is fair in love and war, but I disagree. There is no place for violence against the weak, to oppress, dominate, or discriminate. After revenge porn was circulated (approximately in 2012) by the South

Australian/Victorian Chapter of Comancheros Australian bikers' club in association with the Gypsy Jokers (GER/USA origin), South Australia, and the Bandidos Victoria, AUS, I was first-hand exposed to the predatory behaviour of Australian Army members. Having had no fundamental interactions with defence force members before 2014, I found myself being constantly befriended and pursued by defence personnel after that year. Like the string of police officers that pursued relations with me since 2014, the advances were not asked for nor welcome. I knew I was dealing with an Affray to spread defamation content to distress my life intentionally and maliciously, people conspiring to cause damages, and some with the hope that I would seek the refuge of suicide. A suicide that the creepy government, creepy police, and creepy defence forces wanted to cover up their paedophilia and other vulgar sex crimes. In 2022, I was harassed by persons running the 'justiceformcbride' Instagram page. David McBride is widely recognised as a whistleblower and a former Australian Army service member. Johnny Vance, as he calls himself, is a disturbed man whom David McBride interviewed on his YouTube channel. The fact that Vancey interacted with me via OnlyFans and Instagram is not a coincidence; the fact that seedy defence force personnel had pursued me for years was a plot. A man who publicly calls David McBride his friend and bought him boots, to which David McBride was grateful. Personally, seeing the grateful public Instagram post following a discussion of morality, etc, I couldn't believe that David McBride was accepting the boot handout knowing the deepening association was toxic, but that's his need or greed, not mine. Some people knowingly take the threesome as a reward, while others sidestep cognitive association with the reward. A dog never cares how big the treat is when he sits; he just sits. I also disagreed with David McBride's last court move in the witch hunt prosecution the government held against him, but who am I to talk when I'm not in his boots? In a truth verse lies context. I didn't know who to trust in 2023, but it certainly wasn't going to be seedy defence force personnel, nor men who feel women are a commodity and buy their wives or their friends.

OnlyFans. Suppose you knew me before this police cover-up, in which law enforcement, in direct association with bikers, circulated revenge porn in a character assassination to cover up sex offending against disabled persons and paedophilia. In that case, you'd know you would have never seen me flash my privates, not even at festivals or concerts. As much as sending nudes is a thing in this day and age, my family, partners, and aquatic teaching colleagues were the only people who had ever gotten that personally close to me. The truth is, I would never have taken the steps I have to regain control in defamation, perjury, and an extraordinary emergency, despite the empowering and confidence benefits that can be gained from being comfortable in your own skin, if it weren't for the government cover-up of sex crimes. I've never lacked confidence, yet after a decade of revenge porn, malicious accusations with no basis or facts, and being illegally strip-searched repeatedly, I did lack ownership of my personal dignity. OnlyFans allowed me to gain control over the obsessions people had with me and my life for a short period of time, until, seemingly, some CIA joined some AFP members to cover up sex crimes. I have little to no respect for those guys. Weak men do weak things like sell out to sex, paedophilia, drugs, and a government cover-up. The absolute Hells Angels are supposed to be a said 1% organisation established by ex-veterans, not CIA government dick lickers. You can learn about the gang's establishment online. OnlyFans was not a profitable platform to begin with, as many critics would claim. No one has taken photos for me regarding the OnlyFans platform. When I met photographers modelling in South Australia before OnlyFans, my interaction experiences with photographers were off-putting. They were slimy and schemers. I would never let photographers in Australia photograph me for OnlyFans. I personally think that photographers should be licensed and undergo working with children checks if they want to photograph all ages. That being said, the truth is that I do not advise anyone to sell themselves short of their capabilities in life. Your body is your vessel for your soul, not your be-all and end-all contribution to society, especially in this day and age, where it's easy and counter-productive to a respectful society to treat people as simply objects, not souls. Deep fakes all over the internet are predicted to cater to many pornographic demands as technology develops; people who choose to exploit themselves in the future may heavily regret it. Many OnlyFans users have spoken to the media over the last few years. From a psychological aspect, regret often leads to mental health issues. Regret can be all-consuming, and it can destroy lives, many psychological experts and studies conclude. The flow of effects of regret burdens our societies, increasing mental health issues, suicide, and increased substance abuse. The ego is no way to enlightenment. I had no real choice but to reclaim my power. The narrative that I had choices as I survived during a relentless campaign of lying under oath in an extraordinary emergency is a lie. I could not even gain employment without malicious accusations with no basis or facts disrupting my ability to hold the job. My employment at the Alice Springs Casino is evidence of this fact, perjury, slander – the defamation of sex work spread amongst colleagues and my employer alike. That said, most people are not battling sex industry corruption. I am me and only in a position to legally justify my actions. Your choice is your own, but two minutes of attention is a record of your life – for life. Choose wisely.

A walking lie is a man I met called Timothy Mathison (not the former PM Julia Gillard's partner). He is one of the most unusual people I've met. A self-proclaimed unethical teacher who got engaged to a student he taught Arts to. Chasing her across the world only to label her crazy. When I say unusual, I mean delusional. He had spent seven years floating about on a journey of discovery after his predatory engagement. He has taken numerous spiritual drugs, from Iowaska to having tobacco blown up his nose, etc. I say this, not saying these things are bad, just making a point that too many good things can fuck you up. He drinks Stout - if you buy it for him, as he's never owned a car, had a house, rarely buys food, and has mainly lived in free accommodation since turning fifty years old. Not judging, just facts about a man who calls himself a successful student of art and numerous crafts, who has contributed little to the economy, and is 'in need' grateful for the kindness of others. Not the worst of souls, but definitely a mooch of some type, I call it. During the height of seeking justice for our disabled peers, this man tried to bully me and then denied his actions, calling me crazy. Meanwhile, he had been called delusional the night before and was at least mildly eccentric. Not taking away from the purity of his highly open-minded reality, the cultural stories he shared were clearly somewhat entrancing. When you've been a young backpacker travelling to many places around the globe and a middle-aged person in retirement, you have plenty of stories to tell. With a self-proclaimed background in psychology, he applied his knowledge of conversation to engage with people. Not an uncommon method of fitting in, yet for Tim, sharing common interests was seemingly for the intrigue factor—more of a marketing ploy to suck people in than a basis for life interactions. I don't brag about my psychological understanding personally; that said, it's extensive. From world-leading psychologists to FBI body language experts to literally study material readings, I'm well above the average understanding, especially when it comes to a predator. Most people act as if they genuinely care about others, not just sharing their own interests. I spent numerous days and hours learning about alien interactions with the earth and about a woman who claims to have the highest security clearance in the world. A woman who Tim expects to contact him, as he is a meteor spirit and his work is one of the most important things on this planet, as he puts it. High pedestal, considering it was evident to me that his respect for women and his fellow man, which was of no benefit to him, was nonexistent. A lost soul struggling internally with his inner lack of morality, who should have spent his time travelling in self-assessment regarding preying on his students. Instead, his pride protects him from the devastation of his life going unethically wrong as he delusionally floats about seeking new meaning in life. Unable to separate himself from the facts that he is sixty, unmarried, and has no children. Having to lie to people about his financial woes in hopes that Kim Goguen's universal payout of global assets will end poverty. A woman who pushes fascinating knowledge, hope, and unfortunately thinks life is black and white. Black light and white light – logically flawed views of our expanding, 3D, and beyond, reality.

I had spent hours with Tim when volunteering with him on the farm in 2023, and I was over the pretentious stick up his ass. I called him out on his bullshit finally when he tried to assert authority at the date farm—being deliberately annoying and pushing a door at me during the volunteer period at Desert Date Farm, NT. The facts of logic and life, at times, are lost in Tim's cosmology. Some conversations are amazing, offering dire and truthful insights. Knowledge smashed into the body of a broken man, carried around by his own self-loathing, held up by his pitiful pride.

He wanted to take natural medicine with the Indigenous, yet did not take the opportunity to interact with them, especially when an opportunity presented to learn from Indigenous women. Tim was happy to interact with the women, but they could not teach him what he projected. He wanted the drug, the spiritual medicine, and the feeling of journey that empowered him and made him feel meaningful. In other words, he wasn't being taken onto men's business grounds where, if a woman passed, he may be able to partake or witness rape – this interpretation of the situation is mine after spending much time with the man. He had spoken of being accused numerous times of inappropriately touching women, blaming the close vicinity or cold bones, old age, causing him to fall and grab women's private regions, etc. Women were often liars about sexual assault, he claimed, even though less than ten per cent of reported sexual crimes are falsified. Tim oozed the energy of a sexual predator who was calculating and exhibiting psychotic behaviour. Unable to recognise self-fault and many logical fallacies in his arguments surrounding sexual violence. A clearly sexually deprived man, he spoke of how in cultures he'd associated with, rape was a regular and culturally acceptable standard. Then, he tried to disrespect me while I was studying. Trying to make myself uncomfortable with petty bullying, to which, when I called him out for it, he gaslighted me in defence. Tim accused my interpretation of his actions as a reflection of my Complex PTSD (a comment repeated by the shortest boyfriend in history, Eric, in 2024 to defend his deceitful actions, which he saw no problem with). Following the Date Farm supporting his defamatory claims, he sexually assaulted me, brushing and touching my buttocks deliberately, creating another incident he tried to claim was accidental, and blamed my CPTSD for the outcry. My CPTSD would have seen a far worse reaction than verbal outcrying – this is a fact. All considered, I withheld my instinct reaction and reported the assault to SAPOL police, recording the sexual assault here, and maintained my safety until I left the Date Farm.

Complex PTSD, which no one was aware I carried for twenty-odd years, until the publication of my Autobiographies. PTSD, which has been well-treated and managed for over a decade, where I had been seen as a happy, professional aquatics teacher for most of my career life. What a load of bullshit this man spun in defence of his inconsiderate bullying. A man who for eight years had not worked, had lived off the kindness and generosity of others, who I witnessed with no money eat people out of house and home because he was a man of larger stature, tall, a predatory teacher whose predatory engagement failed. He ran from this ugly truth, claiming it to be change. A person whose financial position could never pay for defamation, who cared not for the justice of disabled persons or my emotional distress. This man, who has relatives who are psychologists who want to drug up women in experimental ancient medicine treatment, has got away with abusing his power as a teacher, committing numerous minor sexual assaults, a pretentious British facade, and eating everyone out of their vegetables for long enough. Here's the consequence of Tim's defamation, aka gaslighting crusade, that labels women witches (so to speak) as he seeks his next mooch prey while taking the opportunity to be a sneaky creep—a man constantly at the servitude of others to survive. In the belief he's on the 'red road' spiritual path. A spiritual path that seemed more akin to that of those who encountered Tim, who tolerated his deliberately eccentric British personality. Maintaining his thick British accent despite having lived globally for several years, he travelled to India, Africa, and America as a backpacker; yet, his theatrical English facade remains his power, his status, and his defining attribute of superiority. Fake as fuck. This man has lived for decades on the generosity of others, who provided him with the basic needs of food and shelter. Yet, his pride always saw it as their service to him on his path. I witnessed a lack of gratitude and genuine respect for others in his behaviour. I detest the misogynist pig after staying around him for months.

I stayed with random Indians via an Airbnb booking, returning to South Australia, migrants here on a working visa who aided and abetted ex police and SAPOL to stalk me almost immediately. The family of three around my age, their child showed a distinct, unhappy demeanour, and entering high school, was forced to stay in the same room as his parents, while the rental house was used mainly to host Airbnb. I noticed the focus on money first with this couple, with earnings taking priority over their child's comfort and genuine family time – as an Airbnb host, I minded my own business. Then I was invited to rent a room in a house with rules posted in nearly every shared room, a home with no lounge or TV, and that was disturbingly quiet at times, considering the four bedrooms were occupied. I was not happy, as I had rented there for only a two-month stay, as I was leaving for the United States as soon as possible. A travel date for my visa, which changed numerous times as the police desperately plotted to try and charge me with entrapment-related bullshit. The family invited me to events, and with us all hanging out casually at times, I thought the stay would be fine – little did I know that the husband was cheating on his wife and was about to ask me to take her somewhere seedy in hopes of alleviating at least his guilt. The husband had already stalked me online without friend requests or follows. I was unsure what to think of this. Then, he stated I knew sex workers – at this point, I thought you didn't get that off my social media (that's for sure!). I felt uncomfortable and was unable to study at the rental during the day, as the husband and even neighbours would walk into the house. Constant knocks on the door. Then I was moved into a different room for subsidised rent. This room was occupied by an Airbnb guest who had already paid for the stay. I spent a week with a random person who had access to thousands of dollars' worth of my property. All because a scabby Indian couple who didn't need to be here communicating with Indians in India for the BHP company wanted to conduct themselves outside of Airbnb standards for extra money. I felt harassed and violated by the actions of this Indian couple and left the Enfield location abruptly after fulfilling volunteering obligations with a corporation connected to the couple. A dodgy church pastor with a Multicultural Community charity front had convinced the Minister of Multicultural Affairs and Tourism, Zoe Bettison MP, to speak at the first-year celebrations. It was at the celebrations that I learned why Zoe Bettison was at this small, unorganised grab at recognition. Clearly encouraged by the SA Premier, Peter Malinauskas, who was linked to the stalking ex-SAPOL police presence within the community centre, and, believe it or not, some of these police personnel were in attendance on the event day. I'm sure Zoe Bettison was innocent enough when accepting the invitation. Clearly, the event organiser and his Indian friends were not innocent in their invitation to me. Leaving the property without prior notice, I left the room key with a Brazilian man of law enforcement background, ensuring the couple could not make defamatory claims about the key. I received no response to my decision to leave until I reached out to the Multicultural Community regarding the event and my absence from Sunday Church Services. Upon doing this, the pastor communicated with the cheating husband, and he sent me a message. I replied with two messages, one to his wife and one via my social media, which both the husband and wife ultimately indulged in.

On social media I wrote something like: "Your husband cheats on you (not with me, I'm very disappointed you'd believe defamation from ex police frankly. I would never) tries to get me to take you to the strippers - when I have Never been in a strip club, with some seedy random chick who likes watching men on men, to elevate his own guilt from cheating. I move and you still don't accept YOU'RE the problem, not me. Wow, just wow.

You're worth more, just saying. Nice doesn't mean stupid."

A text along the lines of, "Thrupthi, you need to sit down and speak to Vasu. I don't want text from him, please. He talked about you being bad at sex and wanted me to take you to a gigolo.

I've researched the sex industry (that's it!), and his conversations stated he's cheated and wanted me to take you to a strip club (which I've never entered before), in front of the Asian Airbnb resident. I am removing myself from the dishonest and venal situation. Best wishes."

Unfortunately, I could not save her from her husband's desires, nor from the consequences of engaging in defamation, criminal conduct, bad dealings, affray, and greed, which breached Airbnb policies. But you can always be honest!

I had just found out my Indian Nanna had passed and was emotionally distressed by this and grieving. In reflection, all actions taken by this Indian couple were vulgar. From their actions to assist stalking, defamation, sexual harassment, and perjury, they are unfit for Airbnb stays, unsafe, and obviously predatory in nature, taking advantage of a vulnerable, grieving individual. Summed up, the enormity of these actions was nothing short of criminal and exploitative.

The Indian couple discussed the 'Greek' man who was interested in me. Encouraging talk about Dave Kyriacou, little did I know that the man who spent A LOT of his time stalking me over the years was now apparently in a relationship while still stalking me as I prepared to fly out to New York. I didn't want to waste time or effort on a fickle man in a relationship. The conversation about

Dave Kyriacou (SAPOL ID 40657) extended beyond sexual harassment at Airbnb. I was attending my family church, my Nanna, who had passed away, church - the St Margaret Anglican Church, Dave Kyriacou, with a substantial Christian presence in Adelaide, where, through his seemingly friend, it was communicated to me that it was Dave Kyriacou's choice between me and some unhappy woman on social media. A comment I made to Dave Kyriacou in 2021, before getting engaged to Travis Paul Enmon Jr., like fuck bald old man, I thought, keep the unhappy bitch, I was doing you a courtesy, not giving you an option. As a family breeding German Shepherds, I was interested in a puppy until I realised that Dave Kyriacou and his false statement (perjury) were still impeding justice for people with disabilities. Taking a six-month-old dog to the USA might not be in the time frame I desired, and the puppy purchase fell through.

Then, furthermore, after spending a month attending St Aidan Anglican Church, avoiding Dave Kyriacou's stalker friends attending St Margaret's, it came to my attention that the man obsessed with me for basically a decade (Constantinos David Kyriacou), who had recently been spending time floating around my presence with his friends, was in a relationship. The SAPOL police officer had displayed an evident lack of self-control over the years. At this point, I could see that he had a clearly non-existent moral compass around me and stopped engaging with his interests that surrounded me. I was kind of shocked that he didn't just move on and be happy. After all, I had been committed to the man that I had wanted to marry in 2021; it was now 2023. We, Travis Paul Enmon Jr, and I were at some point of closure – or at least I was. For me, it was easy to walk away from what doesn't fit my life —relationship-wise, I mean. Once it is over, it's over. People are emotive beings, we feel. Those feelings will subside with time; all feelings do. This is how I felt about Travis, and it was certainly how I thought about the 'Greek', wondering what his next move would be in the background. A power-tripping police officer freemason describes Dave Kyriacou, and, unfortunately for him, after his entrapment and perjury in court following his writing two false statements, he did not scare me in his scorned state or whatever he was attempting at the time. The pointy end of getting close to having sex offender Kurt Gavan Slaven charged for his offending against me as a minor, again.

Ending with a funny truth, well, I find this amusing. Alice Springs Subway had been producing the Chipotle Quesadilla wrap. I'm small in stature, so the size was perfect for grabbing a quick lunch without having to carry my meal around for an hour. I often stopped by the store while in Alice for a bite. In April 2023, the store changed how wraps were made, cutting the wrap's size in half and using half a wrap for the two-dollar and fifty-cent meal. I was mortified when the new employee started making the wrap. The employee knew that I questioned the production, and he assured me that it was correct. A senior member even stepped into his defence, stating this was how Subway wanted them to construct the wrap. A half wrap with a sprinkle of cheese, capsicum, onion, and minimal sauce, for me. At times, I had added avocado at an extra cost—not today; it wouldn't really fit in the half wrap. The standard meal (without added ingredients) would amount to a 50-cent total production cost—that's a handy profit percentage and a clear rip-off for consumers. This is an absolute waste of money when I could get a quick Burger from Hungry Jack's or McDonald's, or even a piece of chicken from KFC for three dollars (as of 2022). So, naturally, I complained to the Subway corporation—happily accepting the scabby wrap that I was given in the store. Only to find out that the scabby was chopped in half, with a less-than-fifty-cent value wrap and barely enough topping to cover it—the ingredients paid for by anyone who got a sub sandwich before me were True!

Chapter Ten
'Real Talk – Australia's Most Infamous
Whistle-blower'

Half of a paedophile protection racket consisting of police, sub-standard bikers, and overall shit humans refuted my whistleblowing with perjury. Everyone else loved me or didn't care about me. Personally, I've never really cared too much about other people's opinions to bother me. Defamation should be compensated; bullshit can be ignored.

"I've interviewed hundreds of whistle-blowers over the years, and hardly any have been successful in both not suffering reprisals and leading to a change in the situation," says Brian Martin, an associate professor in science, technology, and society at the University of Wollongong, in Australia, who has written a how-to for whistle-blowers [see "To Probe Further"]. "Even if you've got everything going your way, it's still hard to be successful."

I was determined to be successful. The truth matters, and when set free, it is like a lion —quite unstoppable. So, I set the beast free against the beast. Only to reveal that the government would rather relish in perjury and try to recklessly endanger my life in hopes of demise or death than to address the sexual misconduct, criminal negligence, rape, and police operations that have played out, leading to numerous deaths. I am lucky to be alive. My Autobiographies highlight the need to always rise against tyranny, write down your experiences, and share the truth with everyone, regardless of relevance, to achieve unequivocal transparency. When corruption is left to fester, like an infected wound, it infects the body to the core.

Assassination - the premeditated act of killing someone suddenly or secretively, especially a prominent person.

The police and government oppression, torts, torturous tactics, psychological warfare, and numerous attempts to push me into the refuge of suicide had been unsuccessful for over a decade. So, police forces desperate to cover up governance sexual crimes against minors and disabled persons attempted to have me seriously injured or worse at times, all based on perjury. In 2023/2024, I was told by some idiots scared that bikers heavily protect the paedophile truth that I'm going to be killed when I get to America – that's the latest plot I thought. Well, if that's the FBI, CIA, AFP, and state counterparts' plan, they'd better send me to the UK like Nicola Gobbo – except no one will be hiding me. I planned to expand my brand at London Fashion Week if the USA police forces were too weak to handle their mess, because going out like that seems lame for bikers or the police to act out, but whatever. How piss weak and pathetic this paedophilia cover-up had become. Bikers doing government dirty work and protecting paedophilia, WTF is that? That's not tough, not 1% nor what any of this should amount to. If I'm being hated for stopping a cover-up of sex crimes, the world is seriously fucked up. Get a life, I thought as one of these twats with a swastika tattoo dribbled his shit. Who the fuck are you to tell me that paedophilia is the new standard for anyone? No one, you're fucking no one here.

In 2023, I found myself forced to stay at a backpacker (as discussed) waiting for torts against Victoria Police (VICPOL) to settle, SAPOL to charge Kurt Slaven, perjury, and affray charges to be acted on by the AFP concerning organised crime and my stress levels to drop from severe emotional distress which had caused two incidents where I fainted in two years. By 2024, it was apparent that everyone was too weak to do fuck all. So, I submitted the four-hundred-plus-page Introduction to UGLY HEROS, The Price of Unlawful Enforcement, as a submission to the Royal Commission of South Australia's inquiry into domestic, family, and sexual violence. The Europe Books edition is slightly inaccurate, but considering the police and government were the defamation, they had enough facts. Cover that up. In response, I was illegally incarcerated for over five (5) months between June and December 2024 at Adelaide Women's Prison (AWP). The government can't cover this shit up, but boy did they try.

After witnessing a year of the AFP aiding and abetting a plot to push me to the refuge of suicide, I put my public disclosure and all of its contents to the South Australian Attorney General, who was commissioned to run the Royal Commission. Submitting via a direct email to the attorney general approximately three weeks before the Royal Commission was due to take official submissions. Fuck you and your plot to assist suicide. I'm never committing suicide to help you cover up your sex crimes, you piss weak rapist, paedophile men. It is irrefutable that both governments received assistance from the Australian Federal Police (AFP), Victoria Police (VICPOL), NSW Police, and SAPOL, at the very least, to delay the settlement of the acknowledged torts in court. No one wanted to see a successful whistle-blower, even if that meant covering up for paedophilia. It had been a year and a half since the Victorian Courts had withheld the acknowledged false-incarceration evidence illegally when I published this e-book. Reece Kershaw, the AFP Commissioner, was irrefutably incapable of performing his duties in the AFP leadership in communicating with state Commissioners. Not acting regarding police organised crime and affray-related offending was intentionally delayed, although the truth was not going away. Law enforcement was incapable of acting to charge sex offenders known to the public in Australia, Australia, purchasing the most child porn years in a row, despite the FBI's help. Law enforcement was a global joke in Australia to anyone in the know – incapable of charging those that had worked for the police force or governance for sex crimes when they were freemasons, in with government, or in the know regarding illegal operations, is a low and frankly embarrassing joke of policing. Despite the magnitude of my whistleblowing, it was the truth. It was impossible to ignore me, even if you wanted to – I refused to be silenced. From my perspective, Reece Kershaw should have stepped down from his position before the National Integrity Commission began operating. However, in 2024, he was rewarded by the government with another term as the AFP Commissioner, which lasted until October 2025. When I watched his reappointment, I knew he needed to get Kurt Slaven charged before this blew up in his face. I knew personally that Dave Kyriacou (SAPOL ID 40657) would not take the blame of perjury lying down, and I knew the cop freemason knew the AFP had their hands dirty in the perjury, covering up Kurt Slaven's sex crimes and the illegal acquisition of my house. I do love a good fight, and in 2024, when I was setting the whistleblowing bombs off in all directions that the battle between SAPOL and the AFP was on and off frequently. Reece Kershaw was not the AFP Commissioner when the Gordon Tearonui Hamm homicide investigation turned into a cover-up; Andrew Colvin was. To me, this shit was on like Donkey Kong. What do you do as the appointed police commissioner, with a Royal Commission bombshell submission already laid on the Attorney-General of South Australia's table —a legal public disclosure of vile governance crimes in South Australia? You ignore it and keep lying, apparently, while locking an innocent victim up in AWP.

I had first-hand witnessed his inability to serve Australians and protect their safety in the face of police criminal negligence. At the same time, this extraordinary emergency saw me in the Northern Territory. Northern Territory police (NTPOL) served under Reece Kershaw's leadership before his promotion to AFP Commissioner under a seedy, paedophile aligned Liberal government. For years, Reece Kershaw had been complicit in oppressive tactics and in passing the buck—the Diffusion of responsibility mentality. In the same month of his re-election (May 2024), I released the non-ambiguous version of UGLY HEROS Autobiography (Europe Books edit). The Australian police force, riddled with people who need to make decisions but are waiting for someone else to act instead. Human psychology holds that the more people involved, the more likely it is that each person will do nothing, believing that someone else in the group will respond, according to psychological studies. Frankly, I was sick of it, and the police had it on record that I would have to be dead for them to succeed in their cover-up. By 2024, there would be no option for a successful cover-up – plausible deniability would be a thing of the past. I eagerly awaited a resolution. No one wants to be the man who allows this cover-up of sex crimes to define his career, surely not I, thought.

In 2023, NTPOL police had engaged in so much perjury that felons made accusations against the AFP, saying they were party to the cover-up. Daniel Jacob Lowe (Born NSW, Australia) mentioned earlier committing four assaults, breaching his parole hundreds of times, as well as defrauding the government by claiming a pension while being paid cash for jobs relating to persons like judges and other public and private associated sectors involved with police. Yet, no one from NTPOL took action to bring him to court. The evidence of criminal negligence was mounting against several state police forces, all claiming the AFP was leading the way to their fate and leading the cover-up of sex crimes in the police force and government. Accusations seeded for years by institutional abuse, torts, perjury – a chain of causation that started with SAPOL. So by 2024, and false incarceration, it was irrefutable that SAPOL was committed to using perjury to cover up sex crimes.

In 2025, from April to 2026, both Kurt Gavan Slaven and David Kyriacou were using a memory post of my beloved dog to try to threaten me with charges and possibly jail time again. A picture of my dog shared with no malicious intent or reference in my mind to two police officers guilty of victimisation, harassment, malpractice, maladministration and further criminal offences.

Whistleblowing sex offences and offenders on a scale of things, the government is desperate to cover up, and things they want to hide absolutely must have been a priority for misappropriation of taxpayers' funds at this time. A level of perjury that is off the charts.

The evidence of police lying under oath, NTPOL actions endangering my life, is irrefutable. Reported to ICAC NT and has apparently been noted as intelligence. Yes, you read that correctly. The police officers involved were not immediately stood down and are yet to be charged with neglectful investigations, criminal negligence, reckless endangerment, torts of harassment and emotional distress, etc. ICAC NT was clearly not fit for purpose, as ICAC SA is in this regard. Police investigating police the obvious problem leading to unprosecuted crimes in instances where it is clear police are engaging in acts of corruption. Endless malfeasance leading to my reporting mounting corruption while enduring extraordinary emergency circumstances of torts, perjury, oppressive and malicious tactics, reckless endangerment, and intentionally abusive conduct.

The screenshot captured messages depict the level of violence and hate that NTPOL had intentionally generated towards my life. I immediately sought a cease-and-desist order, and the legal firm of Bowden McCormack, Lawyers + Advisers, acted quickly to represent me. Unfortunately, NTPOL actions escalated due to perjury, resulting in damages that necessitated court resolution almost immediately. Which legal representation consistently failed to deliver. Inductive reasoning from past experience quickly proved that litigation would arrive too late and would prove both timely and costly. A cover-up had been announced, and character assassination and defamatory allegations were the basis of the cover-up. It's best to carry on from my perspective. The defamatory efforts of oppression via discreditation taken by the police were, from my perspective, self-defeating. I was supposed to be paying for my ex-fiancée, Travis Paul Enmon Jr's lawyer – that's what he kept pestering me for. I had to consider my own survival, business operation expenses, life expenses, and litigation costs. Plus, the half a dozen lawyers saying he's got at least five years to serve, whether I fork out ten thousand US dollars or not. For me, there was no point wasting money I did not have on a lawyer when I could spend two thousand AUD dollars and apply to the high courts for resolution regarding SAPOL charging their sex offender.

Everyone wanted a piece of me and to partake in dehumanisation as opposed to love and humanity. A situation where I could not rely on the kindness of others, as their kindness was rarely genuine.

Police forces' perjury extended to telling many persons I was in trouble, an informant, and under investigation when the truth was that I was a victim. That is simply all I am, a victim – not a criminal, nor an informant, nor a cop. A victim helping themselves, as so many police in the force were corrupt, dehumanising, neglectful, on drugs, not fit to serve, had faced numerous Integrity Investigations, were extorted, or blackmailed, or had committed sex crimes themselves.

Youth Hostel Australia (YHA), part of Youth Hostel International, was where I fully unfolded my Rebellion against plausible deniability and government oppression, despite Bryan Porker being a questionable way to be introduced to the place. Charismatic and well-received, everyone knew Bryan for dealing marijuana. That is how I met Bryan, so in the back of my mind, I always questioned his persona. A drug dealer is not always a nice guy, and I have grown up witnessing the attitudes of such men. They are nice most of the time, but no drug dealer can survive the game without an evil side.

My priority was resolving my whistleblowing and settlement regarding my tort claim against VICPOL (and other police forces), not making friends. I was happy to make friends, and I was also pleased to cut the fat if it was costing me, Barbwire Noose® or Human Rights justice. It mattered not who you were, if you were in the way of justice helping a cover-up of sex offending, big or small, in your disruption, I was willing to allow the truth to take you down. Play the song 'Team' by Australian hip-hop artist Iggy Azalea here. My feelings and actions were clear when Bryan sexually assaulted me; I no longer trusted him or his friends, the management of the YHA. I think my caution is a fair assumption that the Alice Springs YHA managers were going to be loyal to their friend Bryan and not me, especially with a history of dismissal towards male sexual and ethical indiscretions. I was able to move quite quickly, but from this point onward, I noticed clear standoffish body language and a distinct change in Management's behaviour. It quickly became clear to me that management here had been complicit in harassing me. The reception collected phones, illegally, and then handed the initially lost, then stolen by Management phones registered to mainly Indigenous persons, often victims of domestic violence, to felons, drug dealers, and immigrants.

The sicko police forces' criminal negligence led to seeing crimes committed by their felon human resources everywhere. I witnessed a dog being held hostage in 2023. Yes, you read that right. After SAPOL ignored crimes reported against Bryan Porker, he then stole a dog from a woman he claimed was an ex-prostitute in Coober Pedy. He committed two crimes in South Australia, and SAPOL took no action. Stealing the dog not long after he had me hostage, as well as assaulted me. Deprived of liberties like food, I was deprived of numerous meals after his sexual assault, touching my ass, attempting to get under my shorts, the creep attempting digital rape. Knowing he was targeting a whistle-blower, he has a swastika tattoo on his leg – no, he's not the idiot saying I'll be assassinated in the USA. That is another Nazi tattooed fool – I have anti nazi tattooed on my hand and I don't scare easily. Fear is the Root of All Weakness, quoting my brand's slogan, Barbwire Noose. The drug-fuelled Big Brother contestant wannabe turned sex offender drove to an isolated location, in the middle of Australia, to attempt to engage with me sexually. An indigenous property that prohibits trespass. The property, which had no phone signal for like one hundred kilometres, was a premeditated crime, and I was completely vulnerable with little water and no food. While I was sleeping, Bryan Porker assaulted me, feeling and groping my buttocks. Then, he tried to slide his hand under my shorts. I had moved away, upon his attempt to get underneath my clothing, I grabbed his hand and threw it off me. Bryan knew I was not interested in him, and this was a no-go zone. After this vile act, he stole this poor lady's dog, bullying her for months, she claimed, stealing jewellery, borrowing money, and even taking money from her bank accounts, she claims. When she told me about the dog being held hostage by her, she was emotionally distressed. The police in both Western Australia (WAPOL), where Bryan was holding the dog hostage, and South Australia (SAPOL), where the dog was taken from, failed to act and pick up the dog on the day she reported it, which led to further harassment from Bryan. The dog was trapped in an area where it was a target of violence and animal cruelty. The victim expressed that the police did not like her. Personally, I thought that if they liked Bryan more or even allowed a person to be left vulnerable without their family or dog, those people should not be police officers. I had had enough of the dehumanising culture, the lowest of lows standard our law enforcement was, and was willing to stoop to by 2023. Nearing a decade of whistleblowing police over sex crimes, you would be over their bullshit, too. Witnessing, national security risks, sexual and domestic violence, perjury, criminal negligence – you've read the list earlier. The lack of integrity in law enforcement was compromising the safety of our society. Not fit-for-purpose legislation implemented for political gain; governing Australia was out of control. The association laws needed to be abolished. They were never necessary; we have affray laws, conspire laws, etc.

Whistleblowing exposed so much wrongdoing. At three (3) Hayes Street is the location I was supposed to burn down or whatever felons sent to their felon friends. The place is a dump that the owner did not invest fuck all in, even though he's apparently affluent. Spending too much money on cocaine, prostitutes (felons Luke Fulton and Daniel Jacob Lowe claimed), and engaging in privacy breaches against the Tenancy Act, plus violating the Federal Privacy and Security Act. Three (3) Hayes Street, The Gap NT, was barely fit to be leased to tenants. I witnessed much illegal activity while the place was managed by felon and domestic violence offender Luke Fulton. Luke Fulton constantly stating that the army should be harassing the Indigenous community in Alice Springs, NT. The things you are told when people think they are in with the police and above the law are revolting. Oh, what fun whistleblowing has been.

Blackmailed by the Asian invasion cops are always fun to whistle blow – not. The main problem, other than an AFP employee I refused to engage with sexually, called 'Will', whose claim to fame is perjury and being associated with the Rebels biker club, was a man named Jason Canning of NTPOL. 'Will' missed the memo that I do not get involved with cops, and if I do, surprise is on you – it's highly likely my agenda is to report your misconduct or report you for at least creeping on me. Jason Canning is an ugly as fuck, bald old man who gave me his mobile number to communicate regarding an assault incident in 2021. He uses prostitutes, and God knows what he was thinking, but I was not thinking the same; that's for sure. Apparently, this phone number was his private number, and Jason Canning gave it to me under false pretences. Jason Canning has a fetish for Asian women, I learned from his colleague, who was stupid enough to engage with me after I warned him not to. Perjury, I was a Hells Angels prostitute, was mounting, hanging with a cop, created a different mythos – my eyes still on the prize of outing police corruption. Hanging out with a cop was both pleasant and unpleasant, yet productive for whistleblowing. That cop was a New Zealander named John Mills, who thought he was an Angel, me to John – me too, sent directly from God, you fool. As for Jason Canning, the cheap NTPOL crooked cop needed to speak to Dave Kyriacou – I'm well above his pay packet, as I said to Dave the bald SAPOL stalker of 2015. Being a smart aleck here, I'm trying to keep this book light-hearted. I wear designer brands, gold, and diamonds; my own couture; and I am not a cheap girlfriend to chase. God knows what the Asian fetish NTPOL loser wanted. What I do know is that his desire for Asian women makes him incapable of doing his job in the police force of NTPOL Alice Springs. He compromised my life so severely in a cover-up of police using prostitutes, including children, that, for my safety, I needed to make a public announcement about his agenda. Living in an extraordinary emergency circumstance – a cover-up! I had been publicly disclosing facts for years by the time NTPOL jumped onto the cover-up bandwagon. Emailing the facts that "Jason Canning should be sacked and get a job where his sexual desires don't inhibit his job. Leave Northern Territory Police, Fire and Emergency Services, Jason Canning", Tuesday, the ninth of May 2023. This bloke, in all his brothel-using glory, takes the perjury cake with 'Will' of the AFP in the NT, AUS.

Whistleblowing sex offences and offenders on a scale of things, the government is desperate to cover up, and things they want to hide absolutely must be high on the chart, despite the inevitable and overwhelming proof of a cover-up of governance using the sex industry, which includes minors, that was acknowledged in 2020. Police desperately trying to cover up criminal negligence and serious acts of crime, including plots to push persons to the refuge of suicide, psychological warfare, and torture for a decade, is diabolical. I spent many nights uncomfortable. I have constant nightmares; I am often sleep-deprived. I deal with ongoing trauma daily. My complex PTSD is triggered to the point where I am numb to my feelings, like a secret service soldier being tortured for intelligence (from movies).

People are as pathetic, bitter, and cruel in human nature as they can be kind. When you are vulnerable, never forget that, sadly, some people relish in others' misfortune. In Germany, it is called "Schadenfreude" (harm joy) — joy over some harm or misfortune suffered by another.

As is that of these men, slight bragging rights in the depths of ten years of corruption, malicious accusations with no basis or facts as an agenda to cover up governance department sex crimes - basically just as many police Commissioners have generally had short-lived careers in the service of the top job.

Commissioner Malcom Hyde was serving as SAPOL Commissioner when my life was first utilised in South Australia Police Force Operations.

Commissioner Gary Burns was SAPOL's chief Commissioner throughout the Gordon Hamm homicide debacle.

Graham Andrew of VICPOL was the Victoria police chief Commissioner throughout the Gordon Hamm homicide debacle.

Mike Fuller was the Commissioner of NSWPOL when neglectful investigations of sexual crime were conducted in 2019, where I reported a sex offence committed by ex-army personnel Craig Spence. NSWPOL went on to partake in the tort of false incarceration with VICPOL and the Australian Federal Police (AFP) police forces.

Grant Stevens, Commissioner of the South Australia Police Force, was involved in the intentional cover-up of governance sex crimes, including paedophilia.

Shane Paton, Chief Commissioner of Victoria Police Force, who engaged torts of emotional distress, illegal strip searching, and false incarceration, leading to a multi-million dollar tort claim from me and the brand Barbwire Noose®.

Jamie Chalker, Chief Commissioner of the Northern Territory, was involved in torts of harassment/emotional distress, and when NTPOL police officers recklessly endangered my life with intentional and malicious defamation, intending to cause grievous bodily harm.

Ending this chapter on a serious note, one of my biggest tips for whistleblowing is this. Write down precisely what you're going to whistle-blow and add the Public Disclosure Act; activity that is deemed illegal, unethical, or not correct within a public organisation, to the bottom of your work. In Australia, you are automatically protected by copyright law. If you are not located in Australia, please check your legal rights. On International, if copyright demands are via the government, you're about to whistle blow, forget the copyright and remember the legal maxim above – What is first is truest and what comes first in time is best at law.

Share your writing with a dozen friends and family. If you don't know this many people, consider emailing it to relevant citizen bodies, such as historians, retired journalists, or other world activists. Then, report any suspicious activity via integrity agencies if you suspect a cover-up, such as time delays, character assassination (people acting differently towards you), disruptions to bills, or financial matters. Write a book and send your manuscript to publishers.

If your constitutional rights are being violated, my advice is to have the documents (letters, reference numbers, emails) from government integrity departments that are failing to act on blatant criminality, malpractice, and maladministration. Apply via the online portal and email the court's administration to follow up on your application. Attached the letter of response from e.g., ICAC SA, IBAC Victoria, ICAC NT, etc, to your constitutional writs' application. The red tape is ridiculous; your application could be of the utmost importance and seriousness, yet the High Courts will delay it and fuss over a 12-point font. Personally, I see this as a breach of my Human Rights and constitutional writs to demand digital applications and font size specific to the application on grounds of Article 2, Article 6, Article 7, Article 8, especially as a citizen should be entitled to a remedy despite academic abilities, Article 10, Article 27. The fact that Constitutional Writ applications in policy (red tape—not legislation) obstruct justice is a serious flaw in the fairness of our justice system.

The Human Rights and constitutional rights violations outlined in the application; you have the option of employing an International Lawyer, which, if in Australia, I suggest. Most firms receive government funding to provide legal aid. These firms cannot be trusted in their legal capacity to fairly represent you in your quest for justice against the great government dictatorship it calls democracy, until challenged.

The online process is simple, and I suggest that when emailing courts, including the contents of your online application, you also include media outlets, as constitutional writ breaches are of public interest.

To those who challenged the truth's substance and strength, "MENE, God has numbered the days of your kingdom and brought it to an end; TEKEL, you have been weighed ... and found wanting."

Chapter Eleven
'Freemasonry'

"That a man be willing, when others are so too, as far forth as for peace and defence of himself he shall think it necessary, to lay down this right to all things; and be contented with so much liberty against other men, as he would allow other men against himself." - Thomas Hobbes

To be one, ask one – the first mistake in joining is the motivation of power, which overshadows the best of Freemasons.

A person who holds his mortality over money. That learns humanity and teaches charity and humility. A general kind person who is strong in defence of the weak or what is right. A man of a lodge or a wanderer among humanity. A Freemason is a person who wants to wake up every day with an unwavering determination to be better than he was the day before.

I entered Freemasonry in 2015, eager to learn more after inquiring. I was happy to be accepted into a religion with which I felt a genuine connection. More than Christianity or other religions. I was excited to be surrounded by like-minded peers and found peace in the old customs and symbolism. I love everything about Freemasonry except the greed of man and its uncontrollable lust for power. Co-Freemasonry is filled with much less innuendo than the commonly known male-only Freemasonry.

Freemasonry is in my life a cult that found me and, bluntly, is one of the greatest and damaging good vs evil regimes outside of Nazi war times.

Greed, power, lust, delusional belief, and manipulation are not the basis of Freemasonry, but it is the basis for the blind to lead the blind. For years, I suffered through the immoral desires of greed, power, and lust that compromised a society built on morality. The disconnect between what was said and what was done led me to resign from Adelaide South AUS Lodge 406 in 2019. By 2021, the desire to return to this lodge was almost non-existent, yet my desire to contribute to the good I believed freemasons are, overruled the irrational thought that a bad apple ruins the bunch.

"The source of every crime is some defect of the understanding, or some error in reasoning, or some sudden force of the passions. Defect in the understanding is ignorance; in reasoning, erroneous opinion." – Thomas Hobbes, Leviathan.

Freemasonry is truly about four esoteric laws: awareness, clarity, creation, and balance. These concepts provide practical guidelines for personal development and spiritual growth, serving as a blueprint for living a life rich in purpose, wisdom, and harmony. Each law, a universal principle found in many spiritual and philosophical traditions, guides a person through the complexities of life and the mysteries of the universe. Integrating these esoteric laws into daily life is a continuous process of learning, adapting, and growing. Whether you start small, by focusing on one law at a time in life, gradually incorporating these principles into your daily routines, or already practice these laws. Reflection, journaling, engaging, or encouraging like-minded individuals is insight and support for your own inner light. Ultimately, the practice of these laws is about transforming the self and the world. Freemasons and seekers alike are called not only to understand these principles intellectually but also to live them, embodying the virtues of awareness, clarity, creation, and balance in every aspect of life. Through these laws, as lived experience, the esoteric becomes exoteric, and the journey of life enlightenment—a journey for all— is embedded in the broader canvas of human knowledge.

1. Awareness underscores the importance of mindfulness and consciousness in the masonic quest. It is about awakening to the reality that surrounds us, recognising the interconnectedness of all things, and understanding our place within the cosmos. This law encourages people to cultivate a more profound sense of self-awareness, to observe the world with an open mind, and to seek truth beyond the superficial layers of existence. Awareness is the foundation upon which the other esoteric laws rest, serving as a reminder that enlightenment begins with recognising one's own

inner light. Practising the law of awareness involves cultivating mindfulness in everyday activities. It means being fully present in the moment, observing your thoughts and emotions without judgement, and recognising the deeper connections between your inner experiences and the external world. You can enhance your awareness through meditation, reflective practices, or simply by pausing to observe your surroundings intentionally. This heightened state of consciousness enables you to navigate life with greater insight and empathy.

2. The law of clarity focuses on the pursuit of knowledge and understanding with a clear and focused mind. It emphasises the importance of defining one's goals, beliefs, and values with precision. Clarity of thought and purpose enables people to navigate life's challenges with confidence and make decisions aligned with their highest ideals. This law teaches that through clear vision and understanding one can discern the true from the false, the essential from the non-essential – paving the way for meaningful action and personal fulfilment. To apply the law of clarity, start by setting clear intentions in your life. Define your goals, values, and what you stand for with precision and clarity. This could involve writing down your objectives, visualising your desired outcomes, or engaging in self-inquiry to refine your understanding of what truly matters to you. Clarity comes from introspection and the willingness to ask hard questions about your purpose and direction. By doing so, you create

a roadmap that guides your decisions and actions towards a more fulfilling life.

3. The law of creation speaks to the power of intention and the ability to bring one's thoughts and desires into reality. It highlights the Masonic belief in the creative potential of the human mind and spirit, urging people to actively shape their destiny through positive thinking, visualisation, and purposeful action. This law embodies the principle that we are co-creators of our world, responsible for the material and spiritual environments in which we live. The law of creation is brought to life through the power of intention and action. It involves aligning your thoughts, words, and deeds with the reality you wish to manifest. This can be practised by setting specific, actionable goals and taking consistent steps towards achieving them. Creativity, resilience, and a positive mindset are key to this process. The act of creation is not a solitary endeavour but one that invites collaboration and inspiration from the world around you.

4. Balance emphasises harmony and equilibrium in all aspects of life. It recognises that true wisdom and fulfilment come from maintaining a balance between opposing forces: action and reflection, giving and receiving, material success and spiritual growth. This law teaches people the importance of moderation, reminding them that excess in any form can lead to imbalance and discord. Implementing the law of balance requires a conscious effort

to maintain harmony in all facets of life: personal, professional, and spiritual. It is about recognising when to push forward and when to pull back, understanding that rest and activity are both vital to sustained growth. You can practice balance by regularly assessing your priorities, setting boundaries, and being mindful of your physical, emotional, and mental well-being. Embracing balance leads to a more sustainable and rewarding journey through life.

"A peculiar system of morality, veiled in allegory and illustrated by symbols." – This is Freemasonry. For those unaware, the mark of a real freemason is in his 'moral' actions, not his hand signals, jewellery, or stance. Those men are the hated boys' club. I understand your detest if that is how you feel. I honestly think the same way about Freemasonry's bigotry and deceit.

I am on record saying that Freemasons have allowed dues to cloud their judgment. "Money is the root of all evil.", "Fear is the root of all weakness. Power is the root of all delusion." – Those last two quotes are my own spin on the age-old saying.

No one is perfect; a freemason is a man, an imperfect man who works on himself into perfection. The status and status of each man in his membership is his own. The unity of the lodge is founded on brotherly love, for one another and for all who pass through our lives. A freemason is not a man who looks down upon others, but a man who looks down to offer a helping hand. For he knows that life is a gift, what you give, and they furthermore understand that the difference between an everyday man and a freemason is in his charity. To provide if he can, when he can, and to serve humanity, so no human is left behind. A profound belief in God, the great architect of the universe, and a distinct drive to contribute to positive change. True Freemasonry lies within the man, not in the lodge; it is your actions taken when no one is watching, your accountability for mistakes, and your humility in both high and low times.

From the Universal co-freemasonry teachings available online to everyone, I believe this is an excellent explanation of what is meant when we say to bring Light from darkness, or "Ordo Ab Chao" (Latin) - Order from Chaos (English). Much as the operative Masons of old took the rough stone of the natural world and hewed and smoothed it in such a way as to be fit for the construction of elaborate and pristine structures such as cathedrals, so the speculative Masons of today apply the same discipline, and even the metaphor of the builder's tools, to draw forth Order from the Chaos of their own lives and minds. Just as God is said to have made a Light to shine in the darkness which comprehended it not, so are we to be as Lights of knowledge and integrity in the darkness and ignorance of the world, even when it does not understand that Light.

Archaeologist, the late Mr George Smith, of the British Museum, speaking of the cuneiform inscriptions excavated in

Mesopotamia, and the legends which they have preserved of the old Babylonian empire, said:

"With regard to the supernatural element introduced into the story, it is similar in nature to many such additions to historical narratives, especially in the East; but I would not reject those events which may have happened, because, in order to illustrate a current belief, or add to the romance of the story, the writer has introduced the supernatural."

Deus Meumque Jus prominently on Masonic Regalia, of the 32nd and 33rd degrees. Latin phrase Deus Meumque Jus loosely translates to "God and My Right", or more accurately translated to "God and My Moral Rightness." Deus, a familiar Latin word for God, is commonly associated with clothing brands and often heard in Catholic recitations of the Latin Bible. Jus, a word with the Latin root of Justice relating to law, and Memque is a form of Meus, the adjective "my."

The Catholic Church first prohibited Catholics from membership in Masonic organisations and other secret societies in 1738. At least eleven popes have issued pronouncements on the incompatibility between Catholic doctrine and Freemasonry, including Pope Francis (2024). From 1738 until 1983, Catholics who publicly associated with, or publicly supported, Masonic organisations were censured with automatic excommunication. The

Catholic Church continues to prohibit membership in Freemasonry because it believes that Masonic principles and rituals are irreconcilable with Catholic doctrines. The current norm, as stated in the 1983 Declaration on Masonic Associations by the Congregation for the Doctrine of the Faith (CDF), is that "faithful who enrol in Masonic associations are in a state of grave sin and may not receive Holy Communion," and membership in Masonic associations remains prohibited.

The most recent official Holy See documents on the "incompatibility of Freemasonry with the Catholic faith" were issued in 1985 and, in November 2023, by the Dicastery for the Doctrine of the Faith. This initiative arose in response to a question posed by a Filipino bishop recently. A question that led to reaffirming the long-standing position of the Catholic Church that being an active Freemason constitutes a grave sin.

DICASTERIUM PRO DOCTRINA FIDEI

NOTE FOR THE AUDIENCE WITH THE HOLY FATHER - 13 November 2023

The Request of His Excellency, the Most Rev. Julito Cortes,

Bishop of Dumaguete (Philippines)

Regarding the Best Pastoral Approach to

Membership in Freemasonry by the Catholic Faithful.

Recently, His Excellency, the Most Rev. Julito Cortes, Bishop of Dumaguete, after explaining with concern the situation caused in his Diocese by the continuous rise in the number of the faithful enrolled in Freemasonry, asked for suggestions regarding how to respond to this reality suitably from a pastoral point of view, taking into account also the doctrinal implications related to this phenomenon.

Membership in Freemasonry is highly significant in the Philippines; it involves not only those who are formally enrolled in Masonic Lodges but also a large number of sympathisers and associates who are personally convinced that there is no opposition between membership in the Catholic Church and in Masonic Lodges.

To address this issue appropriately, it was decided that the Dicastery would respond by involving the Catholic Bishops' Conference of the Philippines itself, notifying the Conference that it would be necessary to put in place a coordinated strategy among the individual Bishops that envisions two approaches:

(a) On the doctrinal level, it should be remembered that active membership in Freemasonry by a member of the faithful is forbidden because of the irreconcilability between Catholic doctrine and Freemasonry (cf. Congregation for the Doctrine of the Faith,

"Declaration on Masonic Associations" [1983], and the guidelines published by the Catholic Bishops' Conference of the Philippines in 2003). Therefore, those who are formally and knowingly enrolled in Masonic Lodges and have embraced Masonic principles fall under the provisions in the Declaration mentioned above. These measures also apply to any clerics enrolled in Freemasonry.

(b) On the pastoral level, the Dicastery proposes that the Philippine Bishops conduct catechesis accessible to the people and in all parishes regarding the reasons for the irreconcilability between the Catholic Faith and Freemasonry.

Finally, the Philippine Bishops are invited to consider whether they should make a public pronouncement on the matter.

Ex Audientia die 13.11.2023

Franciscus,

Víctor Manuel Card. Fernández

Prefect

The Philippines has a high rate of paedophilia, the Catholic Church, with a long history of paedophilia, and the Philippines is a country of much Christian faith, including many freemasons.

Masonry is a universal morality, applicable to all people regardless of race or creed. It teaches no doctrine, except those truths which tend directly to the well-being of man to achieve better people and 'A Better World'. A simple basis of a happier person in a happier world, and wiser people in a wiser world.

Chapter Twelve
'Opinions and Random Shit'

Opinions are like assholes: everyone has one—these are mine. Plus, Anything but Ordinary random shit.

There's a lot of talk about what happens when we die in life. Some religions believe we will wake up, some in reincarnation, and others that you go to heaven or hell. I think our physical form rots if buried or burns if cremated, and our energy remains aligned with all the space and all the time, encompassing everything we have touched, loved, and hated, as well as everything in between. We make an imprint on this world, big or small. Carrying ancient and new DNA, we dissolve into the atoms and molecules that ultimately define us, because we are all the matter and in all the matter that surrounds us. If we are buried with a tree planted over us, we feed the tree, and therefore some of our energy becomes the tree, and every other being that breathes the air produced by the tree. Life-giving life is the ultimate death.

I do not believe you need to be part of a lodge to be a freemason, and I do not think that every freemason who is part of a lodge is a freemason.

Dogs are often considered better company than humans, yet humans are generally considered better conversationalists than dogs.

An eye for an eye makes the whole world blind. Put two guys who believe in an eye for an eye together and get one to poke out the other's eye, and you will see.

Dirty jokes are better than clean jokes - if you are an adult and not a prude. Dad jokes are the best because everyone can laugh at them.

Swearing is never really appropriate, yet saying please excuse me to someone with a knife as opposed to fuck off out of my way or going in the other direction will probably get you stabbed by the psycho. So, swearing has its purpose.

Reality is, we are all going to die, so never say no to anything that will not kill you. Furthermore, saying yes to something that might kill you but should not and will be fun as fuck is also highly advisable.

Stomping around while bushwalking often deters snakes from your path, as they are creatures of vibration. If you're worried, stomp about and be loud if you can.

The word 'caution' does not mean you cannot do it.

Red cars do not go faster than all other cars, and colour-blind people cannot necessarily see your car, yet we have red stop lights because discrimination is illegal, and it's always been that way. (severe sarcasm here).

Ignorance is not bliss.

Drones should have been registered to their owners upon purchase.

The government does not care about you; they care about money. Voting for people who care about people is the only way to change this fact, and capping government officials' salaries is the only way to do so.

I think a groomer and a paedophile are guilty of the same offence, living their desire in the filth of the offender's eye. The worst predators live in plain sight.

Addiction is defined as not having control over doing, taking, or using something to the point where it could be harmful to you.

Medicinal is defined as referring to a substance or plant that has healing properties.

My honest opinion about OnlyFans, after starting the platform, is that it's a corporation catering to the seedy men that Epstein left behind. If your circle is tight and you post everything disgusting that is demanded. No complaints and no compliance apply. The platform, while providing a level of safety and confidence, also creates a safe space for offenders to stalk and attempt to solicit. Treating users as cash cows, I could see during the witch hunt that was occurring when American and Australian law enforcement focused on my account and banks, interested in the less than 500 Australian dollars that might hit my bank every couple of months. Funds that I mainly invested in Barbwire Noose, running Human Rights Matter billboards, as stated, and for survival.

They is a noun, verb. A word (other than a pronoun) used to identify any of a class of people, places, or things (common noun), or to name a particular one of these (proper noun).

I do not believe in transgender, you can, but I don't. Your spirit is infinite and bound by no gender, but your body, your temple, is designed to function as the mammal you are, with genders to breed. Our DNA holds the truth of our gender, no matter how mangled the body becomes. This is science, not opinion. While you are entitled to believe your own lies, that does not make you right.

"Activism and social engineering ideologies can

Even corrupt the hard sciences. Consider the transgender movement. Seeing gender ideology infect and corrupt his own field, biologist Colin Wright wrote for the Wall Street Journal in 2020; The time for politeness on this issue has passed. Biologists and medical professionals need to stand up for the empirical reality of biological sex. When authoritative scientific institutions ignore or deny empirical facts in the name of social accommodation, it constitutes a grievous betrayal of the scientific community they represent. It undermines public trust in science, and it is dangerously harmful to those most vulnerable." – Tomorrow's World Magazine, page 8 (TomorrowsWorld.org).

The most important thing life has taught me is never to trust anyone entirely, but to trust yourself. Rely on people as little as possible and always be at least truthful to one person in life about you - and make that person YOU. People will misunderstand and mock you, love you, and lust over you. You will be a moment, yesterday's news, tomorrow's bulletin, a superstar, and a loser in someone's eyes all the time. Ensure that you are not trying to be someone else; be humble, confident, and proud of who you are. There is always someone better, and always someone worse, but there is no one else like you. I trust myself entirely, and everyone else I burden with less Trust. Trust is earned by small acts of respect and sincerity. Trusting too easily is just as dangerous as not trusting at all.

Live, Laugh, Love.

Barbwire Noose

1. American podcast media - Grimerica.   2. Meme.   3. NYFW designer opportunity.   4. Farm life.   5. Rock Climbing.   6. Fashion and Sustainability Diploma studies (2024).

The Australian College of the Arts

First Name:	Marcia (Marcia BNoose)
Last Name:	Hobbs
DoB:	25/4/1984
Program:	Diploma of Design (Fashion & Sustainability) - Full-time

LINKS

Socials:

https://www.youtube.com/@Barbwirenoose

https://au.linkedin.com/company/barbwire-noose

https://www.instagram.com/marciabnoose

https://www.instagram.com/barbwirenoose

https://www.facebook.com/BarbwireNoose/

https://mobile.twitter.com/marciabnoose/

https://mobile.twitter.com/barbwirenoose/

Websites:

https://www.marciabnoose.com/

https://www.barbwirenoose.com/

https://www.uglyheros.com.au/marcia-anita-hobbs

https://www.australianfreedomparty.com/

Publications:

Search: Marcia Anita Hobbs and Marcia BNoose for publications available via state, national libraries, and leading bookstores:

https://trove.nla.gov.au/search/advanced/category/books?creator=marcia%20anita%20hobbs

Local – Australia and International interviews and articles:

https://www.brainzmagazine.com/.../barbwire-noose-by...

https://www.brainzmagazine.com/.../empowering-daily...

https://www.brainzmagazine.com/.../secrets-from-the-eco...

https://www.brainzmagazine.com/.../spring-is-almost-over...

https://www.brainzmagazine.com/.../political-prisoner...

https://www.brainzmagazine.com/.../how-to-become-a...

https://issuu.com/lifestyle1media/docs/lifestyle_1_issue_696

https://read.amazon.com.au/?ref_=dbs_p_ebk_r00_pbcb_rnvc00&_encoding=UTF8&asin=B08XJYTGLB

https://borderwatch.com.au/local-news/2018/01/06/lakeswim-lessons-begin/

https://borderwatch.com.au/features/2017/11/21/localfashion-designer-takes-eco-fashion-week/

ANYTHING BUT ORDINARY –

JUDGMENT AND PERCEPTION HAVE NO VALUE HERE.

BOOK NO. 3

ASTRONOMY

Astronomy is the study of everything in the universe beyond Earth's atmosphere.

ASTROLOGY

Taurus, (Latin: "Bull") the zodiacal constellation lying in the northern sky between Aries and Gemini, at about four hours twenty minutes right ascension and 16° north declination. The constellation's brightest star, Aldebaran (Arabic for "the follower"; also called Alpha Tauri), is the 14th brightest star in the sky, with a magnitude of 0.85.

TRAVEL

What do you do when you have nothing else to do, want a holiday, or think the world is calling you?

DICTATORS

Girls in jocks and Boys in panties.

THE FREE WORLD

"People fight today for the same fundamental reasons the Greek historian Thucydides identified nearly 2,500 years ago: fear, honour, and interest." - quote Herbert Raymond McMaster, retired United States Army lieutenant general who served as the 25th United States National Security Advisor from 2017 to 2018.

SEX

The connection between a woman and a man in purity is spiritual— a chakra connection that forms a circle of infinite energy to create life.

POETRY

Poems by yours truly.

POLITICS

The Australian Freedom Party.

TRUTH VS LIES

Be careful what lies you tell about me; some dick heads may be corrected in these books. Defamation is costly.

NATIONAL INTEGRITY AUSTRALIA

A mandamus is typically issued when an officer or an authority, by compulsion of statute, is required to perform a duty. That duty, despite a written demand, has not been performed. In no other case will a writ of mandamus issue unless it be to quash an illegal order.

FREEMASONRY

A man cannot lay down the right of resisting them that assault him by force, to take away his life." - Thomas Hobbes, Leviathan.

OPINIONS AND RANDOM SH*T

Opinions are like assholes: everyone has one—these are mine. Plus, Anything but Ordinary random shit.

An individual is not subject to any civil, criminal, or Administrative liability for making a public interest disclosure. It is an offence to take a reprisal, or to threaten to take a reprisal against a person because of a public interest disclosure (including a proposed or a suspected public interest disclosure). The Federal Court or Federal Circuit Court may make orders for civil remedies (including compensation, injunctions, and reinstatement of employment) If a reprisal is taken against a person because of a public interest disclosure (including a proposed or a suspected public interest disclosure).

It is an offence to disclose the identity of an individual who makes a public interest disclosure.

Public Interest Disclosure Act 2013

No. 133, 2013

(Part 2; Subdivision A—Immunity from liability)

'Barbwire Noose', 'Fear Is The Root Of All Weakness', and the Barbwire logo are All Registered Trademarks.

www.ingramcontent.com/pod-product-compliance
Lightning Source LLC
Chambersburg PA
CBHW051304120626
46547CB00015B/2081